To Dear Shai
Welcome to the
world of Indian
& chines
Cooking

Diwali Pune 2004

BEST OF
CHINESE COOKING

BEST OF
CHINESE COOKING

SANJEEV KAPOOR

In association with Alyona Kapoor

PopulaR prakashan

POPULAR PRAKASHAN PVT. LTD.
35-C, Pt Madan Mohan Malaviya Marg
Tardeo, Mumbai 400 034

First Publication 2003
Second Reprint June 2003
Third Reprint November 2003

(3663)

ISBN-81-7154-911-X

PRINTED IN INDIA
by Vakil & Sons Pvt. Ltd., Industry Manor, 2nd Floor, Worli,
Mumbai and Published by Ramdas Bhatkal
for Popular Prakashan Pvt. Ltd.
35-C, Pandit Madan Mohan Malaviya Marg
Tardeo, Mumbai 400 034.

AUTHOR'S NOTE

Chinese cuisine enjoys the distinction of being the most popular cuisine in the world today. There is hardly any place on this planet where it has been unheard of. In India too it enjoys tremendous popularity not just in the metros but also in the smaller cities where a number of Chinese outlets are doing roaring business. Home-cooked Chinese food however is a recent fad especially since people have realized how easy it is to dish up a Chinese meal.

Many were those who urged me to come out with a book on Chinese recipes. But I wanted to present recipes which were a little different from the ones that have been made popular by the numerous Chinese restaurants dotted all over. It, therefore, took us (my team and myself) a little while to cull out these dishes, try them out and perfect them before presenting them to the ever-growing Chinese food fans.

I must admit that while I was working on this book some unscrupulous elements took advantage of the public demand and came out with a bogus book called "Sanjeev Kapoor's Khazana of Chinese Recipes". This spurious cheap edition mischievously used my picture, my name, my printer's and my publisher's name and address lifted unaltered from my earlier books. Fortunately, the contents were such trash that my discriminating fans who bought this book soon realized that it was not by Sanjeev Kapoor! We have taken certain legal steps but it is this genuine version which I am sure will speak for itself.

I have often been asked if the Chinese food that we eat in India is authentic. In India we definitely make changes to suit our palate and in some cases the changes made are so good and delicious that the same taste is then exported to many countries including the UK, USA and Canada. I know of many restaurants in these countries who serve 'Indo-Chinese' food and do roaring business. To top it all the demand is growing at a very fast pace.

All this furore about Chinese food could make one wonder what is so special about this cuisine. Well, the answer is if one has to put it in one word, it is wholesome. Chinese food has the characteristics of being nutritious, economical, balanced and delicious. It cannot be gainsaid that Chinese food is popular the world over and it can be adapted into our modern lifestyles, as the strong link between diet and health of body, mind and spirit is epitomised in Chinese Cookery. We all desire harmony in our lives and this works on the ancient Taoist principle of Yin and Yang in which balance and contrast are the key. Each Chinese dish reflects a balance of taste, texture, aroma and colour. Be it sweet, sour, pungent, hot, salty or spicy – these six basic flavours are incorporated deftly in all their dishes.

The taste factor is not the only plus point of this delicious cuisine. It scores very high on the health front too. Carbohydrates, such as noodles and rice which provide energy, are served at every meal. Vegetables, providers of vitamins and minerals, also form an integral part of this cuisine. Besides, they are cooked in a manner, such as stir frying or steaming, whereby most of their nutritional values are preserved. In the non-vegetarian fare mostly white meats such as chicken and seafood are used rather than high fat ingredients such as red meats or dairy products, which are either absent or used sparingly.

The great Chinese scholar, philosopher Confucius was known to be a discriminating gourmet too. He liked plain yet wholesome food, which was well cooked and most importantly presented in an appealing manner. An ancient Chinese proverb says "A good meal is eaten first with the eyes, then with the nose and finally with the mouth". The Chinese therefore take their meals very seriously. It has to be a well-presented one where they can savour the aroma and scent as well as the taste.

Like my other books here too each recipe forms part of a menu and serves four portions. Every effort has been made to keep the recipes simple yet interesting and tasty. TASTE IS PARAMOUNT.

Now go ahead and enjoy a home-cooked Chinese meal.

ACKNOWLEDGEMENTS

A. I. Kazi
Aditi Mehta
Afsheen Panjwani
Anand Bhandiwad
Anil Bhandari
Blue Cilantro, Mumbai
Brijesh Lohana
Capt. K. K. Lohana
Chef K. Ganesh
Drs. Meena & Ram Prabhoo
Ganesh Pednekar
Grain of Salt, Kolkata
Harpal Singh Sokhi
Holiday Inn, China Town, Montreal
Jijesh Gangadharan
Jaydeep Chaubal
Jyotsna & Mayur Dvivedi
Legacy of China, Mumbai
Lohana Khaandaan
Lotus Pond, Delhi
Manu Bajaj
Mrs. & Mr. Kalyanpur

Neena Murdeshwar
Nitin Kapoor
Paul Awasthi, Montreal
Pooja & Rajeev Kapoor
Rajesh Choudhary
Rajeev Matta
Rajiv Atri
Rutika Samtani
Sanjiv & Namrata Bahl
Saurabh Malhotra
Shyam Kulkarni
Smeeta Bhatkal
Sunit Purandare
Swapna Shinde
The Yellow Chilli, Jalandhar
The Yellow Chilli, Ludhiana
The Yellow Chilli, Amritsar
The Yellow Chilli, Delhi
The Yellow Chilli, Noida
Tripta Bhagattjee
Uma Prabhu

CONTENTS

RICE & NOODLES

DESSERTS

ANNEXURE

SHRIMP AND CORIANDER SOUP

INGREDIENTS

Shrimps	8 medium sized	Ginger	1 inch piece
Cornstarch	1 tbsp	Oil	1 tsp
Leek	1 inch piece	Fish stock	6 cups
Celery	1 stalk	White pepper powder	½ tsp
Green chilli	1	Ajinomoto	¼ tsp
Coriander leaves	¼ cup	Salt	to taste
Garlic	2-3 cloves	Lemon juice	1 tbsp

METHOD OF PREPARATION

1. Peel, clean, wash and cut shrimps into two lengthways. Blend cornstarch in half a cup of water.

2. Wash, trim and cut leek and celery into julienne. Wash, remove stem and deseed green chilli and cut into julienne.

3. Wash, trim and finely chop coriander leaves. Peel and chop garlic. Wash, peel and finely chop ginger.

4. Heat oil in a wok or a pan, add chopped ginger and garlic and stir fry briefly.

5. Add leek, celery, green chilli julienne and continue to stir fry for half a minute.

6. Add fish stock and bring it to a boil. Reduce heat, add white pepper powder, ajinomoto and salt to taste. Simmer for four to five minutes, stirring occasionally.

7. Add shrimps, and cook for a minute, stirring gently. Stir in blended cornstarch and continue to cook for a minute more. Add finely chopped coriander leaves.

8. Simmer the soup for half a minute and stir in lemon juice and serve piping hot.

Note : *Refer page no.131 for the recipe of Fish Stock.*

HOT AND SOUR VEGETABLE SOUP

INGREDIENTS

Onion	1 small sized	Cornstarch	3 tbsps
Garlic	2-3 cloves	Oil	2 tbsps
Carrot	½ medium sized	White pepper powder	½ tsp
Ginger	1 inch piece	Salt	to taste
Cabbage	¼ small sized	Sugar	½ tsp
Celery	2 inch stalk	Ajinomoto	¼ tsp
Button mushrooms	2	Soy sauce	2 tbsps
Spring onion greens	1	Green chilli sauce	2 tbsps
Bamboo shoot slice	1	Vegetable stock	4-5 cups
Capsicum	½ medium sized	Vinegar	2 tbsps
French beans	4-6	Chilli oil	1 tbsp

METHOD OF PREPARATION

1 Peel, wash, finely chop onion and garlic. Wash, peel, grate carrot and ginger. Wash, trim and finely chop cabbage, celery and mushrooms. Chop the spring onion greens and keep aside.

2 Boil bamboo shoot slice in sufficient water for two to three minutes, drain, cool and finely chop.

3 Wash, deseed and finely chop capsicum. Wash, string and finely chop French beans. Blend cornstarch in half a cup of water.

4 Heat oil in a wok or a saucepan, add chopped onion, garlic, grated ginger and stir-fry briefly. Add chopped celery, carrot, cabbage, bamboo shoot, mushroom, capsicum and French beans.

5 Cook for two to three minutes or until vegetables are almost cooked, stirring continuously. Add white pepper powder, salt to taste, sugar, ajinomoto, soy sauce, green chilli sauce and mix well.

6 Stir in vegetable stock and bring it to a boil. Stir in blended cornstarch and continue to cook for a minute or until the soup thickens.

7 Stir in vinegar, drizzle chilli oil and serve piping hot, garnished with chopped spring onion greens.

Note : *Refer page no.130 for the recipe of Vegetable Stock.*

Chef's Tip : *We have used tinned bamboo shoot slices which are preserved in brine, hence they have to be boiled in water before use.*

BABYCORN AND EGG FLOWER SOUP

INGREDIENTS

Babycorn .... 4-5 small sized	Vegetable stock .... 4½ cups
Spring onion 1	Sweet corn kernels .... 2 tbsps
Garlic .... 2-3 cloves	White pepper powder .... ¼ tsp
Cornstarch .... 2 tbsps	Ajinomoto .... ¼ tsp
Egg... 1	Salt..to taste
Oil .... 1 tbsp	

METHOD OF PREPARATION

1. Wash and thinly slice babycorn. Wash, trim and chop spring onion and reserve some spring onion greens for garnish. Peel and crush garlic.

2. Blend cornstarch in half a cup of water.

3. Separate egg white and keep aside the yolk to use elsewhere. Beat egg white lightly and keep aside.

4. Heat oil in a wok, add crushed garlic and stir fry briefly. Add chopped spring onion and cook for two to three minutes on high heat. Add thinly sliced baby corn and continue to cook for a minute more.

5. Add vegetable stock along with sweet corn kernels and bring it to a boil. Add white pepper powder, ajinomoto and salt to taste.

6. Stir blended cornstarch into the soup, stirring continuously. Bring it to a boil and cook for a minute.

7. Reduce heat and pour a spoonful of beaten egg white into the simmering soup. Let it come up to the surface in the form of a white flower. Repeat till all the beaten egg white is used.

8. Garnish with the reserved spring onion greens and serve piping hot.

Note : *Refer page no.130 for the recipe of Vegetable Stock.*

Chef's Tip : *Use frozen or canned sweet corn kernels for best results. If you are using fresh corn kernels, then precook them till they are soft.*

SOUR AND SPICY CHICKEN SOUP

INGREDIENTS

Chicken breast ..... 1 medium sized	Cornstarch..........................3 tbsps
Mushrooms 6-8	Oil..................................1 tbsp
Carrot.................. ½ medium sized	Soy sauce............................1 tbsp
French beans 5-6	Green chilli sauce..............2 tbsps
Garlic ....2-3 cloves	Ajinomoto.........................¼ tsp
Ginger .... ½ inch piece	White pepper powder .... ½ tsp
Green chillies 2	Salt...................................... to taste
Spring onion............................. 1	Chicken stock ....5-6 cups
Egg... 1	Vinegar .... 2 tbsps

METHOD OF PREPARATION

1. Clean, wash, trim and finely slice mushrooms. Peel, wash and cut carrot into julienne. Wash, string, and cut French beans diagonally into thin diamond shaped pieces.

2. Clean, wash and finely shred chicken breast. Peel and finely chop garlic. Wash, peel and finely chop ginger. Wash, remove stem and finely chop green chillies. Wash, trim, chop spring onion and reserve some spring onion greens for garnish.

3. Break egg into a bowl and whisk lightly. Blend cornstarch in half a cup of water.

4. Heat oil in a wok or a pan, add shredded chicken and stir fry briefly.

5. Add chopped ginger, garlic, green chillies and continue to stir fry for half a minute more. Add chopped spring onion and continue to cook for a minute.

6. Add carrot julienne, sliced mushrooms and French beans. Add soy sauce, green chilli sauce, ajinomoto, white pepper powder and salt to taste. Mix well and stir in chicken stock.

7. Bring to a boil, reduce heat and simmer for three to four minutes. Stir in blended cornstarch and cook for a minute or until the soup thickens, stirring continuously.

8. Stir in whisked egg in a steady stream so that it forms into threads as it cooks.

9. Add vinegar and serve piping hot, garnished with chopped spring onion greens.

Note : *Refer page no.129 for the recipe of Chicken Stock.*

16

SPINACH AND TOFU SOUP

INGREDIENTS

Tofu (bean curd)	100 gms	Vegetable stock	4-5 cups
Spinach	1 medium bunch	Ajinomoto	¼ tsp
Garlic	2-3 cloves	Soy sauce	1 tbsp
Ginger	½ inch piece	White pepper powder	½ tsp
Oil	½ tbsp	Salt	to taste

METHOD OF PREPARATION

1   Cut tofu into quarter inch thick slices and further cut them into one inch triangles.

2   Wash spinach leaves thoroughly under running water, trim and roughly shred. Peel and finely chop garlic. Wash, peel and finely chop ginger.

3   Heat oil in a wok or a pan, add chopped ginger, garlic and stir fry briefly.

4   Stir in vegetable stock and bring to a boil. Reduce heat, add tofu pieces, ajinomoto, soy sauce, white pepper powder, salt to taste and simmer for two to three minutes.

5   Add shredded spinach leaves and continue to cook for a minute, stirring gently. Serve hot.

Note : *Refer page no.130 for the recipe of Vegetable Stock.*

THREE FLAVOUR SOUP

INGREDIENTS

Prawns	6-8	White pepper powder	¼ tsp
Chicken (boneless)	100 gms	Chicken stock	4-5 cups
Spring onion greens	for garnish	Cornstarch	1 tbsp
Black bean paste	1 tbsp	Salt	to taste
Oyster sauce	2 tsps	Chilli oil	1 tbsp
Vinegar	2 tsps		

METHOD OF PREPARATION

1. Peel, devein and wash prawns thoroughly. If they are large, cut each in half lengthways, otherwise leave them whole. Drain and keep aside. Using a sharp knife, thinly slice the chicken.
2. Wash, trim and chop spring onion greens.
3. Mix black bean paste, oyster sauce, vinegar, white pepper powder in half a cup of chicken stock and keep aside.
4. Heat the remaining chicken stock in a wok or a pan, bring it to a boil. Dust sliced chicken pieces and prawns in cornstarch and gently slide them into the boiling stock. Dissolve the remaining cornstarch in half a cup of water.
5. Reduce heat and simmer for about three minutes. Add the blended sauces, dissolved cornstarch, salt to taste and simmer for half a minute.
6. Drizzle chilli oil and serve hot, garnished with chopped spring onion greens.

Note : *Refer page no.129 for the recipe of Chicken Stock.*

TOMATO EGG DROP SOUP

INGREDIENTS

Tomatoes .... 4 medium sized	Oil.. 2 tbsps
Onion .... ½ medium sized	Tomato sauce .... 4 tbsps
Garlic .... 2-3 cloves	Salt.......................................to taste
Ginger (optional) .... 1 inch piece	Sugar.. 1 tsp
Coriander leaves .... 3-4 sprigs	White pepper powder .... ½ tsp
Eggs 2	Ajinomoto.............................¼ tsp
Cornstarch .... 2 tbsps	Vinegar .... 2 tbsps
Vegetable stock .... 4 cups	

METHOD OF PREPARATION

1 Wash and finely chop tomatoes. Peel, wash and finely chop onion and garlic. Wash, peel and finely chop ginger. Wash, trim and finely chop coriander leaves.

2 Break eggs into a bowl and whisk lightly. Blend cornstarch in half a cup of vegetable stock.

3 Heat oil in a wok or a pan, add chopped ginger, garlic and stir fry briefly. Add chopped onion and continue to cook for a minute more.

4 Add tomato sauce, chopped tomatoes and cook on high heat for two to three minutes.

5 Stir in remaining vegetable stock and bring it to a boil. Add salt to taste, sugar, ajinomoto and white pepper powder.

6 Stir in blended cornstarch and cook for a minute or until the soup thickens, stirring continuously.

7 Add vinegar and pour whisked egg in a steady stream, stirring gently to form egg threads. Allow egg to coagulate and come to the top.

8 Serve hot, garnished with chopped coriander leaves.

Note : *Refer page no.130 for the recipe of Vegetable Stock.*

VEGETABLE MANCHOW SOUP

INGREDIENTS

Chinese mushrooms (dried) 2-3	Noodles .... 1 cup
Mushrooms 2-3	Oil................. 2 tbsps + to deep fry
Cabbage...................... ¼ small sized	Cornstarch .... 3 tbsps
Tofu (bean curd) .... 50 gms	Red chilli sauce .... ½ tbsp
Capsicum .... 1 medium sized	Soy sauce .... 2 tbsps
Green chillies 2	White pepper powder .... ½ tsp
Bamboo shoot slices 2	Ajinomoto ....¼ tsp
Carrot................... 1 medium sized	Salt ....to taste
Ginger .... ½ inch piece	Vegetable stock .... 4-5 cups
Garlic ....2-3 cloves	Vinegar 1tbsp
Spring onion 1	

METHOD OF PREPARATION

1. Wash and soak Chinese mushrooms in hot water for fifteen minutes. Drain, wash thoroughly and finely chop.

2. Wash and finely chop mushrooms, cabbage and tofu. Wash, halve, deseed and finely chop capsicum. Wash, remove stem and chop green chillies.

3. Boil bamboo shoot slices in a little water for three to four minutes. Drain completely, cool and chop finely.

4. Wash, peel and finely chop carrot and ginger. Peel and finely chop garlic. Wash, trim, finely chop spring onion and reserve some chopped spring onion greens for garnish.

5. Blanch noodles in hot water, remove and drain well. Heat sufficient oil and deep fry blanched noodles for two minutes or until light brown and crisp. Remove and drain onto an absorbent kitchen towel. Blend cornstarch in half a cup of water and keep aside.

6. Heat two tablespoons of oil in a wok or a pan, add chopped ginger, garlic, green chilli and stir fry briefly. Add chopped spring onion and cook for a couple of minutes.

7. Add chopped mushrooms, cabbage, bamboo shoots, tofu, capsicum, carrot and cook on medium heat, stirring continuously for two minutes.

8. Add chilli sauce, soy sauce, pepper powder, ajinomoto, salt to taste and stir well to mix. Stir in vegetable stock and bring to a boil. Reduce heat and simmer for two to three minutes.

9. Stir in blended cornstarch and cook for two minutes or until the soup thickens, stirring continuously.

10. Stir in vinegar and serve piping hot, garnished with crisply fried noodles and spring onion greens.

Note : *Refer page no.130 for the recipe of Vegetable Stock.*

SWEET CORN VEGETABLE SOUP

INGREDIENTS

Carrot .... ¼ medium sized	Vegetable stock .... 4-5 cups
Cabbage .... ¼ small sized	Sweet corn (cream style) .. 150 gms
Spring onion greens 1	Salt .... to taste
Cornstarch .... 3 tbsps	White pepper powder .... ¼ tsp.
Oil .... 2 tbsps	Sugar .... ½ tbsp
Sweet corn kernels .... ½ cup	Ajinomoto .... ¼ tsp

METHOD OF PREPARATION

1   Wash, peel and cut carrot into small dices. Wash, trim, remove core and finely chop cabbage. Wash, trim and chop spring onion greens.

2   Blend cornstarch in half a cup of water and keep aside.

3   Heat oil in a wok or a pan and add chopped cabbage, carrot and corn kernels. Stir fry for a couple of minutes. Stir in vegetable stock and bring it to a boil.

4   Mix in the cream style sweet corn and continue cooking for two to three minutes or until the cream style corn is mixed well.

5   Add salt, white pepper powder, sugar and ajinomoto. Stir in blended cornstarch, cook on high heat for a minute or until the soup has thickened, stirring continuously.

6   Serve piping hot, garnished with chopped spring onion greens.

Note : *Refer page no.130 for the recipe of Vegetable Stock.*

Chef's Tip : *To make non-vegetarian sweet corn soup, substitute vegetables with chicken or prawns. Finally stir in a whisked egg to give the final touch.*

25

VEGETABLE NOODLE SOUP

INGREDIENTS

Mushrooms 4-5	Vegetable stock .... 4-5 cups
Carrot .... 1 medium sized	Noodles .... 40 gms
Spinach .... 8-10 leaves	Ajinomoto .... ¼ tsp
Capsicum .... ½ medium sized	White pepper powder .... ¼ tsp
Garlic .... 2-3 cloves	Salt .... to taste
Red chilli whole 1	Vinegar .... 1 tbsp
Oil .... 1 tbsp	

METHOD OF PREPARATION

1 Clean, wash, trim and finely slice mushrooms. Peel, wash and cut carrot into julienne.

2 Wash, trim and finely shred spinach leaves. Wash, deseed and cut capsicum into julienne.

3 Peel and crush garlic. Wash, remove stem, deseed and shred whole red chilli.

4 Heat oil in a wok or a pan, add crushed garlic and stir fry briefly. Add mushrooms, carrot, capsicum and stir fry for two minutes. Add shredded red chilli and immediately stir in stock.

5 Bring to a boil, add noodles, reduce heat and simmer for three to four minutes stirring occasionally.

6 Add ajinomoto, white pepper powder and salt to taste. Stir in vinegar and shredded spinach leaves, simmer for a minute and serve hot.

Note : *Refer page no.130 for the recipe of Vegetable Stock.*

Chef's Tip : *Quantity of noodles used in the recipe can be varied depending on your own preference. To make a complete meal of this soup, increase the quantity of noodles and serve in a large bowl.*

VEGETABLE CLEAR SOUP

INGREDIENTS

Carrot .... ½ medium sized
Celery .... 1 stalk
Chinese cabbage .... 4-6 leaves
Spring onion 1
Red capsicum .... 1 medium sized
Snow peas 8-10
Garlic .... 2-3 cloves

Mushrooms 6-8
Vegetable stock .... 4-5 cups
Ajinomoto .... ¼ tsp
Peppercorns (crushed) .... ¼ tsp
Salt .... to taste
Bean sprouts .... ½ cup
Lemon juice (optional) .... ½ tsp

METHOD OF PREPARATION

1   Wash, peel and cut carrot into two lengthways. Cut it further into thin slices. Wash, trim and diagonally slice celery.

2   Wash, trim and dice Chinese cabbage into one inch sized pieces. Wash, trim and slice spring onion. Wash, halve, deseed and cut red capsicum into one inch sized pieces. Wash, string and cut snow peas into two.

3   Peel and crush garlic. Wash, trim and slice mushrooms.

4   Heat vegetable stock in a wok or a pan, add crushed garlic and bring to a boil. Add sliced mushroom, carrot, Chinese cabbage, celery, spring onion, red capsicum, snow peas and cook for two to three minutes.

5   Add ajinomoto, crushed peppercorns, salt to taste and bean sprouts.

6   Stir in lemon juice and serve piping hot.

Note : *Refer page no.130 for the recipe of Vegetable Stock.*

WONTON SOUP

INGREDIENTS

Wonton wrappers 16	Oil.....................................½ tbsp
Cabbage leaves 4-5	White pepper powder..........¼ tsp
Capsicum .... ½ medium sized	Salt.....................................to taste
French beans 2-3	Soy sauce.............................1 tsp
Carrot.................. ½ medium sized	Vegetable stock..............5-6 cups
Spring onion 1	Ajinomoto ....¼ tsp
Garlic................................ 2 cloves	

METHOD OF PREPARATION

1. Wash, trim and finely chop cabbage leaves. Wash, deseed and finely chop capsicum. Wash, string and finely chop French beans. Wash, peel and finely chop carrot.

2. Wash, trim, finely chop spring onion and reserve some chopped spring onion greens for garnish. Peel and finely chop garlic.

3. Heat oil in a wok or a pan, add chopped garlic and stir fry briefly. Add chopped spring onion, capsicum, French beans, carrot, cabbage and continue to cook for a couple of minutes or until the vegetables are cooked, stirring continuously.

4. Add half the quantity of white pepper powder, salt to taste and stir in soy sauce. Cook on high heat for half a minute, remove and cool.

5. Divide the prepared filling into sixteen equal portions. Place a portion of the filling in the center of a wonton wrapper, wet the edges, fold into half diagonally and twist the ends and stick. Repeat to make rest of the wontons.

6. Heat stock in a wok or a pan, add the remaining white pepper powder, ajinomoto, salt to taste and bring to a boil.

7. Reduce heat, gently slide in the prepared wontons and simmer for three to four minutes.

8. Serve piping hot, garnished with reserved chopped spring onion greens.

Note : *Refer page no.130 for the recipe of Vegetable Stock.*

Chef's Tip : *For non-vegetarian soup, change the wonton filling to chicken or prawn and also the stock accordingly.*

CHICKEN GOLD COIN

INGREDIENTS

Chicken mince	250 gms	Cornstarch	2 tbsps
Onion	1 small sized	White pepper powder	½ tsp
Garlic	4-6 cloves	Ajinomoto	¼ tsp
Ginger	½ inch piece	Salt	to taste
Green chillies	2-3	White bread	10 slices
Eggs	2	Sesame seeds (white)	3 tbsps
Soy sauce	1 tbsp	Oil	to deep-fry

METHOD OF PREPARATION

1   Mince chicken once again to get a smooth texture.

2   Peel, wash and finely chop onion. Peel and finely chop garlic. Wash, peel and finely chop ginger. Wash, remove stems and finely chop green chillies.

3   Add chopped onion, ginger, garlic, green chillies, one egg, soy sauce, cornstarch, white pepper powder, ajinomoto and salt to the chicken mince and mix thoroughly.

4   Break the remaining egg into a bowl, whisk lightly. Cut bread slices with a cookie cutter into one and half-inch diameter discs.

5   Brush bread pieces with whisked egg and apply a thick layer of the chicken mixture. Sprinkle sesame seeds generously on the prepared coins and press lightly. Shake off excess seeds and refrigerate for fifteen minutes.

6   Heat sufficient oil in a wok and deep fry the prepared gold coins for two minutes on high heat, stirring frequently. Reduce heat and fry further for three to four minutes or until crisp and golden brown in colour.

7   Remove, drain onto an absorbent kitchen towel and serve hot with a spicy and tangy sauce of your choice.

CHILLI PANEER

INGREDIENTS

Cottage cheese (*paneer*) ... 300 gms	Capsicums ....2 medium sized
Oil .... 2 tbsps + to deep fry	Vegetable stock .... 1 cup
Cornstarch .... 3 tbsps	Salt..to taste
Onion .... 1 medium sized	Soy sauce ....2 tbsps
Garlic ....3-4 cloves	Ajinomoto .... ¼ tsp
Green chillies 6-8	

METHOD OF PREPARATION

1   Cut *paneer* into diamond shaped medium sized pieces. Heat sufficient oil in a wok, roll the *paneer* pieces in one tablespoon cornstarch and deep fry on medium heat until the edges start to turn brown. Remove and drain onto an absorbent kitchen towel.

2   Blend remaining cornstarch in half a cup of water.

3   Peel, wash onion, halve and cut into thick slices. Peel and crush garlic. Wash, remove stem and slice green chillies. Wash, halve, deseed and cut the capsicums into thick strips.

4   Heat two tablespoons of oil in a wok, add crushed garlic and stir fry briefly. Add onion, capsicums, sliced green chillies and continue to stir fry for a couple of minutes.

5   Add fried *paneer* and stir in vegetable stock. Add salt, soy sauce, ajinomoto and mix well.

6   Add blended cornstarch and cook on high heat stirring and tossing until the sauce thickens to coat the *paneer* and the vegetables. Serve hot immediately.

Note : *Refer page no.130 for the recipe of Vegetable Stock.*

CRACKLING SPINACH

INGREDIENTS

Spinach .... 3 bunches
Oil .... to deep fry
Sesame oil .... 1 tbsp
Red chilli flakes .... 1 tsp
Salt .... to taste
Sugar .... 1 tbsp
Toasted sesame seeds .... 1 tbsp

METHOD OF PREPARATION

1 Wash, trim and drain spinach leaves. Pat dry thoroughly with an absorbent kitchen towel and cut into thin strips.

2 Heat sufficient oil in a wok, add spinach leaves and deep fry till crisp. Remove immediately and drain onto an absorbent paper.

3 Heat sesame oil in a wok, add red chilli flakes and immediately add fried spinach. Sprinkle salt, sugar and toasted sesame seeds.

4 Toss well to mix, remove and serve immediately.

Chef's Tip : *Since water content in the spinach is very high, add a little quantity of spinach first to stablize the temperature of the oil before adding the remaining spinach.*

VEGETABLE SPRING ROLLS

INGREDIENTS

Onion .... 1 medium sized	Salt .... to taste
Carrots .... 2 medium sized	Bean sprouts .... ¾ cup
Capsicum .... 1 medium sized	Cornstarch .... 1 cup
Cabbage.................... ½ small sized	**Spring roll wrapper**
Spring onions 2	Refined flour........................ ¼ cup
Oil .... 2 tbsps + to deep fry	Cornstarch .... 1 cup
Soy sauce .... 1 tbsp	Eggs 2
White pepper powder .... ¼ tsp	Salt.......................................to taste

METHOD OF PREPARATION

1   Peel, wash, halve and thinly slice onion. Wash, peel and cut carrots into julienne. Wash, halve, remove stem, deseed and cut capsicum into julienne. Wash, remove core and finely shred cabbage. Wash, trim, halve and thinly slice spring onions along with the greens.

2   Heat oil in a wok or a pan, add sliced onion and carrot, stir fry briefly. Add capsicum and shredded cabbage. Continue stir frying for a minute and add soy sauce, white pepper powder and salt to taste.

3   Add bean sprouts and sliced spring onions along with its greens. Cook for about half a minute, stirring frequently. Remove and cool to bring it to room temperature.

4   Blend one tablespoon of cornstarch in half a cup of water.

5   To make spring roll wrappers, mix cornstarch and flour in a mixing bowl, add eggs and salt with two cups of water and whisk thoroughly. Strain through a fine sieve and leave batter aside for fifteen minutes. Adjust the consistency of batter by adding a little water if required.

6   Heat an eight-inch non-stick pan, brush a little oil and pour a ladleful of batter. Swirl the pan to coat the entire surface of the pan and pour back the excess batter.

7   Cook over medium heat, till edges start curling and peel off or remove spring roll wrapper in one swift motion. Cool and sprinkle a little corn starch. Repeat to make eight to ten wrappers.

8   Divide filling into ten equal portions. Place a portion of filling on one side of the wrapper and roll tightly, folding the sides along and seal the ends with blended cornstarch.

9   Heat sufficient oil in a wok and deep fry two spring rolls at a time in hot oil turning frequently, till they are crisp and golden brown.

10   Drain onto an absorbent kitchen towel and serve hot immediately.

32

DRUMS OF HEAVEN

INGREDIENTS

Chicken wings	24	Ajinomoto	¼ tsp
Garlic	4-6 cloves	Salt	to taste
Spring onion greens	2	Refined flour	¾ cup
Red chilli paste	2 tsps	Cornstarch	¾ cup
Soy sauce	1 tsp	Eggs	2
Vinegar	1 tsp	Oil	6 tbsps+to deep-fry
White pepper powder	½ tsp		

METHOD OF PREPARATION

1 Clean, wash, cut wingtips, remove thin bone and pull the flesh to one end of the thick bone.

2 Peel and grind garlic to a fine paste. Wash, trim and thinly slice spring onion greens.

3 Mix garlic paste, one teaspoon of red chilli paste, sliced spring onion greens, soy sauce, vinegar, white pepper powder, ajinomoto and salt to taste. Marinate the chicken wings in this mixture and leave aside for two hours, preferably in the refrigerator.

4 Meanwhile mix refined flour, cornstarch, eggs, salt, oil, remaining red chilli paste with some water, if required. Whisk thoroughly to make a thick batter of pouring consistency. Rest the batter for fifteen to twenty minutes.

5 Heat sufficient oil in a wok, dip the marinated wings in the batter and deep fry for three to four minutes on medium heat, stirring frequently or until crisp and golden brown.

6 Remove, drain onto an absorbent kitchen towel and serve hot with Sichuan sauce.

Chef's Tip : *Chicken wings made into lollipops, as they are commonly called, can easily be bought from a super market or ask your butcher to make them for you.*

POT ROASTED CHICKEN

INGREDIENTS

Whole chicken with skin	½ kg	Soy sauce	2 tbsps
Honey	3 tbsps	Salt	to taste
Five spice powder	2 tsps	Rice wine vinegar	3 tbsps
Oyster sauce	2 tbsps	Oil	2 tbsps
Red chilli sauce	2 tsps		

METHOD OF PREPARATION

1 Rinse chicken well under running water, pat dry with an absorbent kitchen towel and trim excess fat.

2 Take a large saucepan filled with about six to eight cups of water. Bring it to a boil and remove from heat. Place chicken in hot water, cover and set aside for twenty minutes.

3 Mix honey, five-spice powder, oyster sauce, red chilli sauce, soy sauce, salt to taste and rice wine vinegar.

4 Remove chicken from hot water and pat dry with an absorbent kitchen towel.

5 Brush prepared sauce and spice mix all over the chicken and leave aside to marinate for at least two to three hours. Cut chicken into eight to ten medium sized pieces.

6 Heat oil in a thick bottomed pan, add marinated chicken pieces and cook for a couple of minutes, turning the pieces once. Reduce heat and continue to cook for five to seven minutes or until the chicken is cooked, turning the pieces occasionally.

7 Remove and drain onto an absorbent kitchen towel and serve hot.

8 Alternatively cook the chicken in a preheated oven (180 degrees celsius) for twenty minutes or until it is completely cooked.

Chef's Tip : *Ideally, chicken left in marination overnight under refrigeration gives better results. Personally, I prefer the taste of chicken roasted in the oven.*

DRAGON SEAFOOD ROLLS

INGREDIENTS

For Pancakes
Refined flour ....½ cup
Cornstarch ....¼ cup
Salt ....a pinch
Eggs 2
For Filling
Crabmeat ....1 cup
Shrimps (peeled)................. 8-12
Fish fillet ....100 gm
Spring onion 1
Ginger ....½ inch piece

Garlic .... 2 cloves
Green chilli 1
Egg 1
Oil.............. 1 tbsp + to deep fry
Red chilli paste ....½ tsp
Ajinomoto ....¼ tsp
Soy sauce....................... ½ tbsp
Vinegar .... 1 tbsp
Salt....................................to taste
Bean sprouts ....½ cup

METHOD OF PREPARATION

1 Whisk all the ingredients for the pancake together with enough water to make a thin smooth batter. Strain and set aside for half an hour.

2 Clean, wash, de-vein and roughly chop the shrimps. Wash and cut fish fillet into small dices. Roughly chop crabmeat.

3 Wash, trim and finely chop spring onion. Peel and finely chop ginger and garlic. Wash, remove stem, deseed and finely chop green chilli. Break egg into a bowl and whisk lightly.

4 To make the filling, heat oil in a pan, add chopped ginger, garlic, green chilli and stir fry briefly. Add red chilli paste and chopped spring onion. Sauté for a minute and add the chopped crabmeat, chopped shrimps and diced fish fillet.

5 Sprinkle ajinomoto, soy sauce, vinegar and salt to taste. Mix well and cook till the filling dries up and starts sizzling. Remove, cool and mix bean sprouts.

6 Heat a non-stick pan and brush a little oil. Mix the batter well and pour a ladle full, swirl the pan to coat and pour back the excess batter. Cook on medium to low heat, till the pancake starts leaving the sides of the pan.

7 Remove the pancake carefully and cool. Repeat and make twelve pancakes.

8 Divide the filling into twelve equal portions. Place a portion of the filling at the lower end and roll, while folding the sides along. Brush the edges with egg and seal tightly. Repeat with all the pancakes and keep the rolls ready.

9 Heat sufficient oil in a wok and deep fry the prepared rolls in moderately hot oil, turning the rolls frequently until crisp and golden brown in color. Remove and drain onto an absorbent kitchen towel.

10 Serve hot with a dipping sauce of your choice.

Chef's Tip : *You can substitute the seafood with any of your favourite meats or vegetables.*

CREAM CORN

Sweet corn (cream style) .... 1 tin (400 gms)

Cornstarch .... 10 tbsps + to dust

Salt...to taste

White pepper powder .... ½ tsp

Oil................................. to deep fry

METHOD OF PREPARATION

1   Mix together sweet corn, cornstarch, salt, white pepper powder and one cup of water and cook till it is thick.

2   Spread it on a greased plate, smoothen the top and keep it in the refrigerator till it sets properly.

3   Cut into square or diamond shaped pieces and dust with cornstarch. Heat oil and fry these pieces till golden brown.

4   Serve hot.

HONEYED CHICKEN WINGS

INGREDIENTS

Chicken wings	16-20	Red chilli flakes	2 tbsps
Cornstarch	½ cup	Salt	to taste
Garlic	2 cloves	Lemon juice	1 tsp
Oil	2 tbsps + to deep fry	Honey	4 tbsps
Light soy sauce	2 tbsps	Toasted sesame seeds	1 tbsp
Hoisin sauce	2 tbsps		

METHOD OF PREPARATION

1 Clean, wash and pat dry chicken wings. Blend two tablespoons of cornstarch in one cup of water and reserve the rest for dusting the chicken wings. Peel and crush garlic.

2 Heat sufficient oil in a wok or a pan, dust chicken wings with remaining cornstarch and deep fry turning frequently, for about four to five minutes. Remove chicken wings and drain onto an absorbent kitchen towel.

3 Heat two tablespoons of oil in a wok or a pan, add crushed garlic and stir fry briefly. Immediately add soy sauce, hoisin sauce, chilli flakes and salt to taste.

4 Add fried chicken wings and stir in the blended cornstarch. Cook on medium to high heat for a minute, stirring continuously.

5 Reduce heat and stir in lemon juice and honey, mix well and cook further on medium heat for a couple of minutes.

6 Sprinkle toasted sesame seeds and serve hot.

OPEN STEAMED DUMPLINGS

INGREDIENTS

Chicken mince .... 1¼ cups	Sesame oil .... 1 tsp
Green chillies 2	Salt .... to taste
Spring onions 2	Peppercorns (crushed) .... ½ tsp
Ginger .... 1 inch piece	Wonton wrappers 16

METHOD OF PREPARATION

1 Wash, remove stems, deseed and finely chop green chillies. Wash, trim and finely chop spring onions along with the greens. Wash, peel and grind ginger into a paste.

2 Combine all the ingredients except the wonton wrappers in a mixing bowl. Cover with a cling wrap and refrigerate for half an hour.

3 Brush a wonton wrapper with a little water, place about two teaspoons of the prepared filling on it. Gather the edges together and squeeze lightly to seal, leaving the top a little open.

4 Repeat the same with all the wonton wrappers, using up all the filling.

5 Arrange the dumplings in small batches in a steamer without touching each other and steam for about fifteen minutes or until the filling is cooked.

6 Serve hot with a hot and spicy sauce.

Chef's Tip : *If you cannot get a Chinese steamer, use a cooker in the same way as you would to steam idlis or dhokla.*

PANEER LOLLIPOP

INGREDIENTS

Cottage cheese (*paneer*) ... 200 gms	White pepper powder .... ½ tsp
Ginger .... 1 inch piece	Ajinomoto .... ¼ tsp
Garlic .... 4-6 cloves	Salt .... to taste
Onion .... 1 medium sized	Cornstarch .... 2½ tbsps
Green chillies 2-3	Babycorn .... 16 pieces
Coriander leaves .... ¼ bunch	Oil .... to deep-fry
Potatoes .... 3 medium sized	Refined flour .... ¼ cup
Soy sauce .... ½ tbsp	

METHOD OF PREPARATION

1   Grate *paneer* and mash well. Peel, wash and finely chop ginger and garlic. Peel, wash and finely chop onion. Remove stems, wash and finely chop green chillies. Wash, trim and finely chop coriander leaves. Boil potatoes in sufficient water. Drain, cool, peel and mash boiled potatoes.

2   Add chopped ginger, garlic, green chillies, onion, coriander leaves, soy sauce, white pepper powder, ajinomoto, salt, mashed potatoes and cornstarch to the mashed *paneer* and mix thoroughly.

3   Divide the *paneer* mixture into sixteen equal portions. Roll each portion into a smooth ball and pierce the thicker side of a babycorn into the *paneer* ball. Press the *paneer* ball lightly between your palms to secure it firmly on the babycorn.

4   Heat sufficient oil in a wok, roll the prepared lollipops in flour, shake to remove excess flour and deep fry for three to four minutes on medium heat, or until crisp and golden brown, turning occasionally.

5   Remove, drain onto an absorbent kitchen towel and serve hot with Sichuan sauce.

Chef's Tip : *You can also use wooden ice cream stick instead of babycorn.*

GOLDEN FRIED JUMBO PRAWNS

INGREDIENTS

Jumbo prawns 12-16	Ajinomoto .... ¼ tsp
Garlic .... 4-6 cloves	Salt .... to taste
Oyster sauce (optional) .... 2 tbsps	Refined flour .... ¾ cup
Lemon juice .... 1 tbsp	Cornstarch .... ½ cup
Soy sauce .... 1 tsp	Baking powder .... ¼ tsp
White pepper powder .... ½ tsp	Oil .... ¾ cup+to deep fry

METHOD OF PREPARATION

1. Wash, remove shell and devein prawns retaining the tip of the tail. Pat dry prawns thoroughly with an absorbent kitchen towel.

2. Wash and grind garlic to a fine paste.

3. Mix garlic paste, oyster sauce, lemon juice, soy sauce, white pepper powder, ajinomoto and salt to taste. Apply this mixture liberally on the prawns and leave aside to marinate for two hours, preferably in the refrigerator.

4. Mix refined flour, cornstarch, baking powder, oil, salt to taste and three-fourth cup of water. Whisk thoroughly to make a batter of pouring consistency and set aside for twenty minutes.

5. Heat sufficient oil in a wok, dip marinated prawns in the batter by holding the tail and deep fry for two to three minutes on medium heat, turning frequently or until crisp and golden brown in colour.

6. Remove, drain onto an absorbent kitchen towel and serve hot with a sauce of your choice.

Chef's Tip : *This batter needs to be whisked thoroughly so that the oil used in the batter is incorporated well. You can also increase the quantity of oil in the batter for a crisper result.*

PAPER WRAPPED CHICKEN

INGREDIENTS

Chicken breasts (boneless) ... 300 gms	Soy sauce .... 2 tbsps
Red chillies whole 2-3	Sugar .... 1 tsp
Spring onions 8-10	Salt .... to taste
Ginger .... 1 inch piece	Egg 1
Five spice powder .... ¼ tsp	Rice/Butter paper ...... as required
Dry sherry (optional) .... 2 tbsps	Oil .... for frying

METHOD OF PREPARATION

1   Clean, trim and cut chicken breasts into half inch sized pieces.

2   Soak red chillies in half a cup of hot water for ten minutes. Drain, remove stem and cut into julienne. Wash, trim and finely chop spring onions.

3   Peel and finely chop ginger. Mix chicken pieces with five spice powder, dry sherry, chopped ginger, red chillies, soy sauce, sugar, salt to taste and chopped spring onions. Rest the marinated chicken for an hour, preferably in the refrigerator.

4   Whisk egg with a pinch of salt and keep. Cut sixteen pieces of rice paper/butter paper measuring six-inch by six-inch.

5   Brush each piece of paper lightly with the whisked egg mixture and place two tablespoons of marinated chicken on one side of the paper. Drizzle some marinade on the chicken and roll tightly. Finally press or twist the two ends to seal.

6   Heat oil in a wok or deep pan and deep fry the paper wrapped chicken in hot oil for two to three minutes. Drain well and serve immediately, with a spicy sauce of your choice.

Chef's Tip : *Let your guests unwrap the chicken on the table to savour the full aroma of the dish.*

BEST OF CHINESE COOKING

45

STEAMED CHICKEN BUNS

INGREDIENTS

For Dough

Refined flour	3 cups
Sugar	3 tsps
Dried yeast	1½ tsps
Salt	1 tsp

For Filling

Chicken breast	250 gms
Garlic	2 cloves
Green chilli	1
Spring onions	2
Cornstarch	2 tsps
Oil	2 tbsps
Soy sauce	½ tbsp
Sugar	½ tbsp
Salt	to taste

METHOD OF PREPARATION

1 Dissolve sugar in one cup of warm water and sprinkle dried yeast. Stir and leave for ten minutes or until the mixture is frothy.

2 Sift flour and salt together in a bowl. Stir in the yeast mixture with half a cup of warm water to make a soft and pliable dough.

3 Knead by hand for about two to three minutes. Cover with a moist cloth and leave in a warm place until it doubles in size.

4 For the filling of the buns, clean, wash and pat dry chicken breasts. Roughly chop chicken into very small dices.

5 Peel garlic and crush lightly. Wash, remove stem, deseed and finely chop green chilli. Wash, peel and chop spring onions.

6 Blend the cornstarch in three tablespoons of water and keep aside.

7 Heat oil in a pan, add chopped garlic, chopped spring onions and stir fry briefly. Add chopped chicken, chopped green chillies, soy sauce, sugar and salt to taste.

8 Stir well over high heat, stir in blended cornstarch and thicken the chicken mixture. Remove and cool.

9 Knock back the dough to remove the air bubbles and knead for about a minute.

10 Divide the dough into sixteen equal portions, flatten each portion a bit. Place a spoonful of the filling in the center of each, gather the sides, seal and roll into a ball.

11 Line the steamer compartment with butter paper and arrange the buns without touching each other. Leave it for fifteen to twenty minutes or until the buns double in size.

12 Cover and steam over gently simmering water for fifteen minutes or until cooked. Serve immediately.

CRISPY WONTONS

INGREDIENTS

Wonton wrappers	24	Garlic	4-6 cloves
Cabbage	½ small sized	Oil	2 tbsps + to deep fry
Capsicums	2 medium sized	White pepper powder	½ tsp
French beans	8-10	Salt	to taste
Carrots	2 medium sized	Ajinomoto	¼ tsp
Spring onions	2	Soy sauce	1 tsp

METHOD OF PREPARATION

1 Wash, trim, remove core and finely chop cabbage. Wash, halve, deseed and finely chop capsicums. Wash, string and finely chop French beans. Wash, peel and finely chop carrots. Wash, trim and finely chop spring onions. Peel and finely chop garlic.

2 Heat two tablespoons of oil in a wok or a pan, add chopped garlic and stir fry briefly. Add chopped spring onion, capsicums, French beans, carrots and cabbage and continue to stir fry for a couple of minutes more, stirring and tossing continuously.

3 Add white pepper powder, salt, ajinomoto, soy sauce and cook for half a minute. Remove and cool.

4 Divide prepared filling into twenty-four equal portions. Place a portion of the filling in the center of a wonton wrapper, wet the edges with a little water, fold into half diagonally, twist the ends and stick.

5 Repeat this process to prepare all the wontons. Heat sufficient oil in a wok, add prepared wontons and deep fry for two to three minutes or until crisp and golden brown in colour. Remove and drain onto an absorbent kitchen towel.

6 Serve hot with Sichuan sauce.

SESAME CORN TOAST

INGREDIENTS

Corn kernels (fresh) .... 1 cup	Soy sauce .... ½ tbsp
Capsicum .... 1 medium sized	Cornstarch .... ¼ cup
Onion .... 1 medium sized	White pepper powder .... ½ tsp
Ginger .... 1 inch piece	Ajinomoto .... ¼ tsp
Garlic .... 4-6 cloves	Salt .... to taste
Green chillies 2-3	Bread slices 8
Coriander leaves .... ¼ cup	Toasted sesame seeds .... ½ cup
Potatoes .... 3 medium sized	Oil .... to deep-fry

METHOD OF PREPARATION

1   Wash, drain thoroughly and finely mince corn kernels. Wash, halve, deseed and finely chop capsicum. Peel, wash and finely chop onion. Peel, wash and finely chop ginger and garlic.

2   Wash, remove stems, deseed and finely chop green chillies. Wash, trim and finely chop coriander leaves. Boil potatoes in sufficient water, drain, cool, peel and mash them.

3   Add chopped onion, ginger, garlic, green chillies, coriander leaves, capsicum, soy sauce, two tablespoons of cornstarch, pepper powder, ajinomoto and salt to the minced corn and mashed potatoes. Mix thoroughly.

4   Blend the remaining cornstarch in half a cup of water. Cut bread slices with a round cookie cutter to one inch diameter pieces.

5   Brush the bread pieces with blended cornstarch and apply a thick layer of the corn mixture and smoothen with wet hands. Sprinkle sesame seeds generously on the pieces and press lightly. Shake off the excess seeds and refrigerate for fifteen minutes.

6   Heat sufficient oil in a wok and deep fry the prepared pieces for two to three minutes, or until crisp and golden brown in color, turning occasionally.

7   Remove, drain onto an absorbent kitchen towel and serve hot with a sauce of your choice.

48

SICHUAN CHILLI POTATOES

INGREDIENTS

Potatoes............. 4-5 medium sized	Sichuan peppers (optional) ... 8-10
Oil .... 2 tbsps + to deep fry	Red chilli paste.....................1 tsp
Cornstarch .... 3 tbsps	Soy sauce...............................1 tsp
Onion .... 1 medium sized	Sugar....................................½ tsp
Garlic..............................5-6 cloves	Salt..to taste
Spring onion greens 1	Vinegar .... 1 tbsp
Red chillies whole 4-5	

METHOD OF PREPARATION

1 Wash, peel and cut potatoes into ten to twelve thick wedges. Soak in cold water for half an hour. Heat sufficient water and par boil potato wedges, drain and cool.

2 Heat oil in a wok, dust the par boiled potatoes with two tablespoons of cornstarch and deep fry for two minutes or until golden brown and completely cooked and crisp. Remove and drain onto an absorbent kitchen towel or paper.

3 Peel, wash, halve and slice onion. Peel and finely chop garlic. Wash, trim and roughly chop spring onion greens. Blend the remaining one tablespoon of cornstarch in quarter cup of water.

4 Heat two tablespoons of oil in a wok, break whole red chillies into two and stir fry briefly. Immediately add Sichuan peppers, sliced onion, chopped garlic and continue to stir fry.

5 Stir in the red chilli paste blended in a quarter cup of water, soy sauce, sugar and salt. Stir fry briefly. Add fried potatoes and toss to heat through.

6 Stir in blended cornstarch, toss well to mix and add vinegar. Stir fry for half a minute and serve garnished with chopped spring onion greens.

Chef's Tip : *You can also use leftover finger chips for this recipe.*

BEST OF CHINESE COOKING

51

◀ *Almond Vegetables (Page 52)*

ALMOND VEGETABLES

INGREDIENTS

Almonds	15-20	Coriander leaves	1 tbsp
Cottage cheese *(paneer)*	100 gms	Cornstarch	2 tbsps
Carrot	1 medium sized	Oil	2 tbsps
French beans	4-6	Vegetable stock	2 cups
Capsicum	1 medium sized	Salt	to taste
Cauliflower	¼ medium sized	White pepper powder	¼ tsp
Button mushrooms	6-8	Ajinomoto	¼ tsp
Ginger	½ inch piece	Chilli oil	1 tbsp
Garlic	3-4 cloves		

METHOD OF PREPARATION

1. Soak almonds in hot water for fifteen minutes, drain and peel. Cut *paneer* into diamond shaped one inch sized pieces.

2. Wash, peel and cut carrot into diamond shaped one inch sized pieces. Wash, string and cut French beans into diamond shaped one inch sized pieces.

3. Wash, halve, remove stem, deseed and cut capsicum into diamond shaped one inch sized pieces.

4. Wash and cut cauliflower into small florets. Wash and cut mushrooms into quarters.

5. Peel, wash and finely chop ginger and garlic. Wash, trim and finely chop coriander leaves. Blend cornstarch in half a cup of water.

6. Heat oil in a wok, add chopped ginger, garlic and stir fry briefly. Add carrot, French beans, cauliflower, mushrooms and stir fry briefly. Add vegetable stock and bring it to a boil. Reduce heat and simmer for a couple of minutes.

7. Add almonds, *paneer*, capsicum, salt, white pepper powder and ajinomoto. Stir in the blended cornstarch and cook on high heat for about two minutes or until the sauce thickens, stirring occasionally.

8. Stir in chopped coriander leaves, drizzle chilli oil on top and serve hot.

Note : *Refer page no.130 for the recipe of Vegetable Stock.*

CHILLI CAULIFLOWER

INGREDIENTS

Cauliflower	1 ½ medium sized	Spring onion greens	2-3
Cornstarch	½ cup	Soy sauce	2 tbsps
Salt	to taste	Tomato sauce	2 tbsps
Oil	2 tbsps+to deep fry	Vegetable stock	1 ½ cups
Garlic	3-4 cloves	Vinegar	2 tbsps
Ginger	1 inch piece	Sugar	1 tsp
Onion	1 medium sized	Ajinomoto	¼ tsp
Capsicum	1 medium sized	White pepper powder	¼ tsp
Green chillies	4-6		

METHOD OF PREPARATION

1 Wash, trim and cut cauliflower into medium sized florets. Soak the florets in warm salted water for ten to fifteen minutes, drain and pat dry.

2 Blend two tablespoons of cornstarch in half a cup of water. Mix in the remaining cornstarch with cauliflower florets and salt to taste. Sprinkle a little water and mix thoroughly.

3 Heat oil in a wok and deep fry the coated cauliflower florets for three to four minutes or until they are crisp and light golden brown. Drain and remove onto an absorbent kitchen towel.

4 Peel, wash and finely chop garlic and ginger. Peel, wash and thinly slice onion. Wash, remove stem, deseed and cut capsicum into julienne.

5 Wash, remove stem and thinly slice green chillies. Wash, trim and thinly slice spring onion greens.

6 Heat two tablespoons of oil in a wok and stir fry the chopped ginger and garlic briefly. Add sliced onion, green chillies, capsicum julienne and stir fry for a minute.

7 Add soy sauce and tomato sauce. Stir and add the vegetable stock. Bring to a boil, reduce heat and simmer for two minutes.

8 Add fried cauliflower florets, vinegar, sugar, ajinomoto, white pepper powder and salt to taste. Stir in the dissolved cornstarch and cook stirring continuously till the mixture thickens and coats the cauliflower florets.

9 Garnish with sliced spring onion greens and serve hot.

Note : *Refer page no.130 for the recipe of Vegetable Stock.*

MIXED VEGETABLE MANCHURIAN

INGREDIENTS

Cabbage	1 medium sized	Garlic	4-6 cloves
Carrot	1 medium sized	Celery	2 inch stalk
French beans	8-10	Green chillies	3
Springs onions	3 medium sized	Cornstarch	3 tbsps
Capsicum	1 medium sized	Oil	2 tbsps
Salt	to taste	Soy sauce	2 tbsps
Refined flour	¼ cup	Sugar	1 tsp
Cornstarch	¼ cup	Ajinomoto	½ tsp
Oil	to deep fry	Salt	to taste
Sauce		Vegetable stock	2 ½ cups
Ginger	1 inch piece	Vinegar	1 tbsp

METHOD OF PREPARATION

1 Trim, wash and grate cabbage. Wash, peel and grate carrot. String the French beans, wash and finely chop. Wash, trim and finely chop spring onions. Reserve chopped greens for garnish.

2 Wash, halve, remove stem, deseed and finely chop capsicum. Wash, remove stems and finely chop green chillies.

3 Peel and finely chop the garlic and ginger. Wash and finely chop the celery. Blend three tablespoons of cornstarch in one cup of water.

4 Mix grated cabbage, carrot and chopped French beans in a bowl and thoroughly rub in one teaspoon of salt. Add chopped spring onion, capsicum, refined flour and one-fourth cup of cornstarch. Mix thoroughly. Shape into lemon sized balls.

5 Heat sufficient oil in a wok and deep fry vegetable balls in small batches for three to four minutes on medium heat or until golden brown. Drain and remove onto an absorbent kitchen towel.

6 Heat two tablespoons of oil in a wok or a pan and stir fry the chopped ginger and garlic briefly. Add the chopped celery, chopped green chillies and stir fry briefly.

7 Add soy sauce, sugar, ajinomoto and salt to taste. Stir in vegetable stock and bring to a boil.

8 Stir in blended cornstarch and cook for a couple of minutes or until the sauce starts to thicken, stirring continuously.

9 Add the fried vegetable balls, vinegar and mix well. Serve hot, garnished with chopped spring onion greens.

Note : *Refer page no.130 for the recipe of Vegetable Stock.*

Chef's Tip : *If you want to serve it dry without the sauce, reduce the stock to one cup and cornstarch in the sauce to one and half tablespoons only.*

BEST OF CHINESE COOKING

54

SICHUAN TOFU AND VEGETABLES

INGREDIENTS

Tofu (bean curd) .... 100 gms	Cornstarch .... 2 ½ tbsps
Oil ....2 tbsps + to deep fry	Red chilli paste .... 1½ tbsps
Broccoli .... ½ medium sized	Sichuan peppers (optional) .. 8-10
Snow peas 8-10	Sugar .... 1 tsp
Mushrooms 4-6	Salt ....to taste
Garlic .... 4-6 cloves	Ajinomoto .... ¼ tsp
Celery .... 1 stalk	Vegetable stock .... 2 cups
Spring onions 2	Vinegar ....1 tbsp

METHOD OF PREPARATION

1   Wash and cut tofu into one-inch sized pieces, deep fry in hot oil, remove, drain and keep aside.

2   Wash, trim and cut broccoli in small florets. Wash and cut snow peas into two.

3   Clean, wash, trim and slice mushrooms. Peel and crush the garlic. Wash, trim and finely chop celery. Wash and chop spring onions. Blend cornstarch in one cup of water.

4   Heat two tablespoons of oil in a wok or a pan, add chopped garlic, spring onions and celery, stir fry briefly. Add red chilli paste, Sichuan peppers, sugar, salt and ajinomoto. Add half a cup of vegetable stock and cook for a minute.

5   Add broccoli florets, snow peas, mushrooms and stir fry briefly. Stir in remaining vegetable stock and cook on a high heat for a couple of minutes.

6   Stir in blended cornstarch. Cook on medium heat for a minute or until the sauce starts to thicken, stirring occasionally.

7   Add fried tofu pieces and vinegar, stir well and serve hot.

Note : *Refer page no.130 for the recipe of Vegetable Stock.*

BEST OF CHINESE COOKING

GARLIC VEGETABLES WITH CASHEWNUTS

INGREDIENTS

Cashewnuts	12-16	Garlic	10-12 cloves
Bamboo shoots	2-3 slices	Cornstarch	2 tbsps
Carrot	1 medium sized	Corn kernels	½ cup
Snow peas	8-10	Oil	4 tbsps
Chinese mushrooms (dried)	3-4	Star anise	1
Capsicum	1 medium sized	Ajinomoto	¼ tsp
Broccoli	¼ medium sized	White pepper powder	¼ tsp
Spring onions	2	Salt	to taste

METHOD OF PREPARATION

1   Broil or dry roast cashewnuts in a pan on medium heat for two to three minutes or until it is light brown in colour and crisp, tossing continuously.

2   Soak bamboo shoot slices in two cups of hot water for ten to fifteen minutes. Drain well and cut into one inch sized pieces. Wash, peel, halve and cut the carrot into one inch sized pieces. Wash, string and cut each snow peas into two.

3   Soak Chinese mushrooms in sufficient hot water for ten to fifteen minutes. Drain well and cut into quarters. Wash, halve, remove stem, deseed and cut capsicum into one inch sized pieces.

4   Wash, trim and cut broccoli into medium florets. Wash, trim and slice spring onions. Chop spring onion greens and reserve for garnish. Peel and finely chop garlic. Blend cornstarch in one cup of water.

5   Boil sufficient water and cook corn kernels for two to three minutes or until almost cooked. Drain and keep aside.

6   Heat oil in a wok, add star anise, chopped garlic and stir fry briefly. Add sliced spring onion, carrot, Chinese mushrooms and continue to stir fry for a couple of minutes more.

7   Add bamboo shoots, capsicum and broccoli. Cook for a minute on high heat, stirring continuously.

8   Stir in one and a half cups of water and bring to a boil. Reduce heat and add ajinomoto, pepper powder, salt and mix well. Add snowpeas, corn kernels and cook on high heat, stirring continuously for a minute more.

9   Stir in blended cornstarch and toasted cashewnuts. Cook for a minute or until the sauce thickens. Serve hot, garnished with chopped spring onion greens.

FRIED EGGPLANT

INGREDIENTS

Eggplants .... 4 medium sized	Soy sauce...........................2 tbsps
Salt ....to taste	Ajinomoto .... ½ tsp
Oil .... 4 tbsps	Refined flour .... 6 tbsps
Spring onions 2	**Batter**
Garlic ....2-3 cloves	Cornstarch .... ¾ cup
Green chilli 1	Eggs...2
Soya granules .... ½ cup	Salt....................................to taste
Chilli oil............................ 2 tbsps	Oil.......................................to fry

METHOD OF PREPARATION

1 Wash and cut eggplant lengthways. Sprinkle some salt and leave aside for ten minutes. Drain, wash and make criss cross slits on the inside of eggplant. Brush a little oil and bake in a preheated oven (180 degree Celsius) for fifteen to twenty minutes or until the eggplant is cooked. Remove from the oven and cool.

2 Wash, trim and finely chop spring onions. Peel and finely chop garlic. Wash, remove stem, deseed and finely chop green chilli. Soak soya granules in two cups of hot water for twenty minutes. Drain and squeeze out excess water.

3 Scoop eggplants with a spoon without tearing the skin. Chop scooped out eggplant and keep aside.

4 Heat chilli oil in a wok or a pan, add garlic and stir fry briefly. Add chopped green chilli and spring onions and cook for a minute on medium heat. Add soya granules, chopped eggplant, soy sauce, ajinomoto and salt to taste.

5 Stir fry for two to three minutes or until the moisture has evaporated. Divide the mixture into eight equal portions and stuff the eggplant shells. Dust the stuffed eggplants with flour and keep aside. Mix cornstarch, eggs, salt and whisk to make a smooth and thick batter.

6 Heat sufficient oil in a flat pan, dip stuffed eggplant in the cornstarch batter and shallow fry on medium heat for two to three minutes or until crisp and golden brown turning once carefully

7 Remove, drain onto an absorbent paper and serve hot.

HOT HONEY PANEER

INGREDIENTS

Cottage cheese (*paneer*) ... 300 gms	Honey .... 3 tbsps
Oil ....2 tbsps + to deep fry	White pepper powder .... ½ tsp
Cornstarch..........................4 tbsps	Red chilli paste.............. 1 ½ tbsps
Noodles .... 100 gms	Ajinomoto .... ¼ tsp
Onion .... 1 medium sized	Salt .... to taste
Garlic...............................6-8 cloves	Vegetable stock.................... 2 cups
Tomato sauce .... 4 tbsps	Red chilli flakes .... 1 tbsp
Soy sauce .... 1 tbsp	

METHOD OF PREPARATION

1. Cut *paneer* into pieces of half inch thickness. Heat sufficient oil in a wok, roll the *paneer* pieces in two tablespoons of cornstarch and deep fry on medium heat until the edges start to turn brown. Remove and drain onto an absorbent kitchen towel.

2. Boil noodles in sufficient water until almost cooked. Remove and drain thoroughly. Reheat the oil and deep fry noodles until crisp. Remove and drain onto an absorbent kitchen towel. Blend remaining cornstarch in half a cup of water.

3. Peel, wash onion, cut into quarters and separate the layers. Peel and crush garlic. Blend tomato sauce, soy sauce, honey, white pepper powder, red chilli paste, ajinomoto and salt to taste in one cup of vegetable stock.

4. Heat two tablespoons of oil in a pan, add crushed garlic and stir fry briefly. Add onion and continue to stir fry for half a minute. Stir in the sauce and spices mix and remaining vegetable stock. Cook on high heat for two minutes, stirring occasionally.

5. Stir in blended cornstarch and continue to cook for a couple of minutes or until the sauce starts to thicken. Add fried *paneer* pieces and cook on medium heat for half a minute or until the sauce coats the *paneer* pieces. Serve hot on a bed of crispy fried noodles topped with red chilli flakes.

Note : *Refer page no.130 for the recipe of Vegetable Stock.*

SINGAPORE SWEET GARLIC VEGETABLES

INGREDIENTS

Chinese cabbage .... ¼ small sized	Red chilli paste .... 1 tsp
Red chillies whole 2	Tomato sauce .... 2 tbsps
Capsicum .... 1 small sized	Ajinomoto .... ¼ tsp
Red capsicum .... ½ small sized	Sugar .... 3 tbsps
Yellow capsicum ..... ½ small sized	Salt .... to taste
French beans 4-6	Vegetable stock .... 2 cups
Button mushrooms 6	Oil .... 4 tbsps
Garlic .... 12-14 cloves	Vinegar .... 1 tbsp
Cornstarch .... 2 ½ tbsps	Sesame oil .... 1 tbsp

METHOD OF PREPARATION

1   Wash, trim and cut Chinese cabbage into one inch sized pieces. Remove stems and break whole red chillies into two. Wash, halve, deseed and cut capsicum into one inch sized pieces. Wash, deseed and cut red and yellow capsicum into one inch sized pieces.

2   Wash, string and diagonally cut French beans into one inch sized pieces. Clean, wash and cut mushrooms into quarters. Peel and finely chop garlic.

3   Blend cornstarch in one cup of water. Mix red chilli paste, tomato sauce, ajinomoto, sugar and salt to taste in one cup of vegetable stock.

4   Heat oil in a wok or a pan, add broken red chillies, chopped garlic and stir fry briefly.

5   Add mushrooms, French beans and stir fry for a minute. Add Chinese cabbage and stir in the sauce and spice mix and remaining vegetable stock.

6   Cook for four to five minutes and stir in the blended cornstarch. Add capsicum, red and yellow capsicums and continue to cook for two to three minutes or until the sauce starts to thicken and coats the vegetables well.

7   Stir in the vinegar, sesame oil and serve hot.

Note : *Refer page no.130 for the recipe of Vegetable Stock.*

SWEET SOUR PANEER AND PINEAPPLE

INGREDIENTS

Cottage cheese (*paneer*) ...... 300 gms	Tomato sauce .... 3 tbsps
Oil ....2 tbsps+to deep fry	Sugar ....2 tbsps
Cornstarch .... 4 tbsps	Pineapple juice .... ½ cup
Onion .... 1 medium sized	Ajinomoto .... ¼ tsp
Ginger......................... ½ inch piece	White pepper powder .... ½ tsp
Garlic ....2-3 cloves	Salt.................................to taste
Capsicum ....: 1 medium sized	Vegetable stock............. 1 ½ cups
Pineapple slice 1	White vinegar .... 3 tbsps

METHOD OF PREPARATION

1   Cut *paneer* into diamond shaped medium sized pieces. Heat sufficient oil in a wok, roll the *paneer* pieces in two tablespoons of cornstarch and deep fry on medium heat until the edges start to turn brown. Remove and drain onto an absorbent kitchen towel.

2   Peel and wash onion, cut into quarters and separate the layers. Peel and finely chop ginger and garlic. Wash, halve, deseed and cut capsicum into one inch sized pieces. Cut pineapple slice into one inch sized pieces. Blend remaining cornstarch in one cup of water.

3   Blend tomato sauce, sugar, pineapple juice, ajinomoto, white pepper powder and salt to taste in one cup of vegetable stock.

4   Heat two tablespoons of oil in a wok or a pan, add chopped ginger, garlic and stir fry briefly. Add onion and continue to stir fry for a minute.

5   Stir in sauce and spice mix, remaining vegetable stock and blended cornstarch. Cook for a couple of minutes or until the sauce starts to thicken, stirring continuously.

6   Add fried *paneer*, pineapple and capsicum. Cook for a minute more or until the sauce coats the *paneer* pieces. Stir in vinegar and serve hot.

Note : *Refer page no.130 for the recipe of Vegetable Stock.*

CHINESE STIR FRIED VEGETABLES

INGREDIENTS

Button mushrooms	4-6	Spring onions	2
Tofu (bean curd)	100 gms	Cornstarch	1 tbsp
French beans	4-6	Oil	4 tbsps
Chinese cabbage	¼ small sized	Salt	to taste
Broccoli	½ medium sized	Ajinomoto	½ tsp
Capsicum	1 medium sized	Sugar	1 tsp
Babycorn	4-6 small sized	Light soy sauce	2 tbsps
Carrot	1 medium sized	White pepper powder	½ tsp
Spinach	10-12 leaves	Toasted sesame seeds	1 tbsp
Garlic	6-8 cloves		

METHOD OF PREPARATION

1   Clean, wash and cut mushroom into quarters. Wash and cut bean curd into eight to ten pieces, soak in hot salted water for five minutes, drain and keep aside. Wash, string and diagonally cut French beans into one inch sized pieces. Trim, remove core, wash and cut Chinese cabbage into one inch sized pieces.

2   Wash, trim and cut broccoli into small florets. Soak the florets in warm salted water for fifteen minutes, drain and keep. Wash, halve, remove seeds and cut capsicum into diamond shaped one inch sized pieces.

3   Wash and diagonally slice baby corn. Wash, peel, halve and diagonally slice carrot. Wash and tear spinach leaves into two. Peel and crush garlic. Wash, trim and slice spring onions and reserve some sliced greens for garnish. Blend cornstarch in one cup of water.

4   Heat oil in a wok, add garlic and sliced spring onion, stir fry briefly. Add carrot, baby corn, mushrooms, broccoli, continue to stir fry and add French beans, capsicum and Chinese cabbage and cook for two to three minutes.

5   Stir in one cup of water and simmer for a couple of minutes. Add salt, ajinomoto, sugar, soy sauce and pepper powder.

6   Add spinach leaves and tofu. Stir in blended cornstarch, toss well to thicken the sauce and coat all the vegetables. Sprinkle toasted sesame seeds and serve hot, garnished with reserved spring onion greens.

CHILLI GARLIC OKRA

INGREDIENTS

Ladyfingers (okra) .... 500 gms	Oil .... 2 tbsps + to deep-fry
Capsicum .... 1 medium sized	Soy sauce .... 1 tbsp
Green chillies 3-4	Ajinomoto .... ½ tsp
Garlic .... 6-8 cloves	White pepper powder .... ½ tsp
Onion .... 1 medium sized	Salt .... to taste
Cornstarch .... 4 tbsps	Red chilli flakes .... 2 tbsps

METHOD OF PREPARATION

1 Wash, pat dry and trim the tip and the crown of the ladyfingers. Wash, halve, remove stem, deseed and cut capsicum into strips.

2 Wash, remove stems and diagonally slice green chillies. Peel and finely chop garlic. Peel, wash and slice onion.

3 Sprinkle two tablespoons of cornstarch on ladyfingers and mix well. Blend the remaining cornstarch in one cup of water. Heat sufficient oil in a wok and deep fry ladyfingers until golden brown and crisp. Remove and drain onto an absorbent kitchen towel.

4 Heat two tablespoons of oil, add chopped garlic and stir fry briefly. Add sliced onion, green chillies and capsicum and sauté for two to three minutes or until the onion is translucent.

5 Add soy sauce, ajinomoto, white pepper powder, salt and blended cornstarch. Cook for a couple of minutes or until it thickens, stirring continuously.

6 Add fried ladyfingers and toss well to mix. Sprinkle red chilli flakes and serve hot.

HUNAN VEGETABLES

INGREDIENTS

Lotus root, fresh 1	Chinese cabbage leaves 4-6
Capsicum .... ½ medium sized	Soy sauce .... 1½ tbsps
Red capsicum......¼ medium sized	Red chilli paste .... 1 tbsp
Yellow capsicum ..... ¼ medium sized	Ajinomoto .... ¼ tsp
Cucumber .... 1 small sized	Salt.................................to taste
Ginger.......................1 inch piece	Vegetable stock. ....1 cup
Garlic ....3-4 cloves	Cornstarch .... 2 ½ tbsps
Celery................................ 1 stalk	Oil..............to deep fry +2 tbsps
Onion .... 1 small sized	Bean sprouts ....:.¼ cup
Oyster mushrooms 3-4	Vinegar .... 1 tbsp
Spinach........................... 6-8 leaves	Roasted cashewnuts ....2 tbsps

METHOD OF PREPARATION

1 Scrub, wash thoroughly and thinly slice lotus root. Parboil in sufficient salted water for five minutes, drain and remove. Wash, deseed and cut capsicum into one inch sized pieces. Wash, deseed and cut red and yellow capsicum into one inch sized pieces.

2 Wash, peel, halve, scoop out the seeds and cut cucumber into one inch sized pieces. Peel and finely chop ginger and garlic. Wash, trim and finely chop celery.

3 Peel, wash, cut onion into quarters and separate each layer. Soak oyster mushrooms in sufficient hot water for fifteen minutes. Drain and slice them. Wash, trim and tear spinach and Chinese cabbage leaves into smaller pieces.

4 Mix soy sauce, red chilli paste, ajinomoto and salt to taste in half a cup of vegetable stock. Blend cornstarch in the remaining vegetable stock.

5 Heat sufficient oil in a wok and deep fry parboiled lotus root for a minute. Drain and remove onto an absorbent kitchen towel.

6 Increase heat and deep fry cucumber, capsicums and onion for half a minute. Drain and remove onto an absorbent kitchen towel.

7 Heat two tablespoons of oil in a wok or a pan, add chopped ginger, garlic, celery and stir fry briefly. Stir in the blended soy sauce and spice mix. Bring it to a boil.

8 Add fried vegetables, spinach and cabbage leaves, bean sprouts, oyster mushrooms, vinegar and mix well. Stir in blended cornstarch and cook for a minute or until the sauce coats the vegetables. Serve hot, garnished with roasted cashewnuts.

Note : *Refer page no.130 for the recipe of Vegetable Stock.*

BEST OF CHINESE COOKING

EGGPLANT YU XIANG STYLE

INGREDIENTS

Eggplants..............8-10 small sized
Salt ....to taste
Cornstarch ....3 tbsps
Oil .... to deep fry
Sauce
Spring onions 2
Green chillies 2
Garlic ....2-3 cloves
Ginger ....1 inch piece

Hoisin sauce .... 1 tbsp
Sugar......................................½ tsp
Malt vinegar .... 1 tbsp
Ajinomoto...........................¼ tsp
Soy sauce......................1 ½ tbsps
Salt.. to taste
Cornstarch............................ 1 tbsp
Oil...2 tbsps

METHOD OF PREPARATION

1   Wash, pat dry and quarter the eggplants lengthways. Sprinkle salt and leave aside for fifteen minutes. Wash, drain well and pat dry with an absorbent kitchen towel. Add salt to taste and three tablespoons of cornstarch to the eggplant and mix lightly.

2   Heat sufficient oil in a wok or pan and deep fry the eggplants until they are crisp and light golden brown. Drain and remove onto an absorbent kitchen towel.

3   Wash, trim and finely chop spring onions. Wash, remove stem, deseed and slit green chillies. Peel and finely chop garlic and ginger.

4   Blend the hoisin sauce with sugar, vinegar, ajinomoto, soy sauce, and salt to taste. Blend one tablespoon of cornstarch in one cup of water.

5   Heat oil in a wok, add chopped garlic, ginger, slit green chillies and stir fry briefly. Add chopped spring onion and continue to stir fry for a minute more.

6   Add blended sauce and the seasoning mix and stir in blended cornstarch. Cook till it starts to thicken and add fried eggplant. Toss well and serve hot.

HOT GARLIC BABYCORN

INGREDIENTS

Babycorn 20-25	Tomato sauce.................... 4 tbsps
Cornstarch .... 4 tbsps	Vinegar .... 1 tbsp
Oil .... 3 tbsps + to deep fry	Red chilli paste .... 2 tbsps
Capsicum .... ½ medium sized	Hot black bean paste .... 1 tbsp
Red or yellow capsicum	Sugar... 1 tsp
.... ½ medium sized	Salt .... to taste
Red chillies whole 2-3	Vegetable stock.................... 1 cup
Spring onion 1	Sesame oil............................. 1 tbsp
Onion .... 1 medium sized	Red chilli flakes .... 1 tbsp
Garlic .... 10-12 cloves	

METHOD OF PREPARATION

1. Wash, trim and cut babycorn diagonally into one and half inch sized pieces. Sprinkle two tablespoons of cornstarch and mix well. Sprinkle two tablespoons of water if you find it too dry.

2. Heat sufficient oil in a wok and deep fry babycorn for three to four minutes or until crisp. Drain and remove onto an absorbent kitchen towel.

3. Wash, remove stem, deseed and cut capsicum into diamond shaped half inch sized pieces. Wash, remove stem, deseed and cut red or yellow capsicum into diamond shaped half inch sized pieces. Remove stem and break red chillies into two.

4. Wash, trim and finely slice spring onion. Peel, wash and cut onion into quarters and separate each layer. Peel and finely chop garlic. Blend two tablespoons of cornstarch in one cup of water.

5. Heat oil in a wok or pan, add dried red chillies, chopped garlic and stir fry briefly. Add tomato sauce, vinegar, red chilli paste, hot black bean paste, sugar and salt to taste. Stir in vegetable stock and continue to cook on high heat for a minute.

6. Add both capsicums, onion, spring onion and cook for a couple of minutes more. Stir in the blended cornstarch and cook till it starts to thicken.

7. Add deep fried babycorn and toss well to coat. Drizzle sesame oil, sprinkle red chilli flakes and serve hot.

Note : *Refer page no.130 for the recipe of Vegetable Stock.*

THREE TREASURE VEGETABLES

INGREDIENTS

Tofu (bean curd) .... 150 gms	White pepper powder .... ½ tsp
Cornstarch .... 2 ½ tbsps	Sugar .... 1 tsp
Broccoli .... 1 medium sized	Ajinomoto .... ¼ tsp
Carrots .... 2 medium sized	Salt .... to taste
Garlic .... 2-3 cloves	Rice wine (optional) .... 2 tbsps
Oil .... 2 tbsps	Vegetable stock .... 2 cups
Light soy sauce .... 1 tbsp	Five spice powder .... ¼ tsp

METHOD OF PREPARATION

1 Wash, drain and cut tofu into one inch sized pieces. Blend cornstarch in one cup of water.

2 Wash, trim and cut broccoli into medium sized florets. Wash, peel and cut carrots into quarter inch thick slices. Peel and finely chop garlic.

3 Heat two tablespoons of oil in a wok, add chopped garlic and stir fry briefly.

4 Add broccoli, carrot slices and continue to stir fry for a couple of minutes more.

5 Add light soy sauce, white pepper powder, sugar, ajinomoto, salt to taste and rice wine. Mix well and stir in the vegetable stock. Cook on high heat for a minute, stirring continuously .

6 Stir in blended cornstarch and cook for a minute or until the sauce starts to thicken. Add cut tofu and five spice powder, mix well and serve hot.

Note : *Refer page no.130 for the recipe of Vegetable Stock.*

BRAISED SICHUAN CHICKEN

INGREDIENTS

Chicken breasts (boneless) ... 500 gms	White pepper powder .... ½ tsp
Black mushrooms 6-8	Rice wine (optional) .... 1 tbsp
Ginger .... 1 inch piece	Salt .... to taste
Spring onions 2	Ajinomoto .... ¼ tsp
Cornstarch .... 1 ½ tbsps	Chicken stock .... 1 cup
Red chillies whole 4-5	Oil .... 2 tbsps
Hot soy bean paste .... 2 tsps	Chilli oil .... 2 tbsps
Sugar .... 1 tsp	

METHOD OF PREPARATION

1   Clean, wash and cut boneless chicken into one inch sized dices. Pat dry the chicken pieces thoroughly with a clean kitchen towel. Soak black mushrooms in sufficient hot water for fifteen minutes. Drain and cut them into quarters.

2   Wash, peel and thinly slice ginger. Wash, trim and cut spring onions into one inch long pieces. Blend cornstarch in half a cup of water.

3   Remove stems and break whole red chillies into two. Mix hot soy bean paste, sugar, white pepper powder, rice wine, salt to taste and ajinomoto with chicken stock.

4   Heat two tablespoons of oil in a wok or in a pan. Add sliced ginger, broken red chillies and stir fry briefly. Add diced chicken, spring onions, mushrooms and continue to stir fry for a couple of minutes more.

5   Stir in the sauce and spice mix, cook on medium heat for a minute and stir in the blended cornstarch.

6   Cook on high heat for half a minute or until the sauce coats chicken pieces well, stirring and tossing continuously.

7   Drizzle chilli oil and serve hot.

Note : *Refer page no.129 for the recipe of Chicken Stock.*

CHICKEN MANCHURIAN

INGREDIENTS

Chicken (boneless) .... 400 gms	Capsicum .... 1 medium sized
Egg 1	Green chillies 3-4
Cornstarch .... 6 tbsps	Spring onion greens 2
Salt ....to taste	Oil .... 4 tbsps + to deep fry
Soy sauce....................... 2 tbsps	Ajinomoto .... ¼ tsp
Onion................ 1 medium sized	Chicken stock .... 2 cups
Garlic..........................8-10 cloves	Vinegar ....2 tbsps
Ginger .... 2 inch piece	

METHOD OF PREPARATION

1 Clean, wash and cut the boneless chicken into finger sized pieces. Mix egg, four tablespoons of cornstarch, salt to taste, one tablespoon soy sauce into chicken pieces. Leave aside for half an hour.

2 Peel, wash and slice onion. Peel and finely chop the garlic and ginger. Wash, halve, deseed and cut capsicum into strips.

3 Wash, remove stem and roughly slice green chillies. Wash, trim and finely chop spring onion greens. Blend remaining cornstarch in one cup of water.

4 Heat sufficient oil in a wok and deep fry marinated chicken for two to three minutes. Remove and drain onto an absorbent kitchen towel.

5 Heat four tablespoons of oil in a wok or a pan, add chopped ginger, garlic and stir fry briefly.

6 Add onion, green chillies and continue to stir fry for a minute. Stir in remaining soy sauce, ajinomoto, chicken stock and salt to taste. Bring to a boil.

7 Stir in blended cornstarch and cook for a minute more or until the sauce starts to thicken, stirring continuously.

8 Add fried chicken pieces and capsicum and cook for a couple of minutes. Stir in vinegar and serve hot, garnished with chopped spring onion greens.

Note : *Refer page no.129 for the recipe of Chicken Stock.*

Chef's Tip : *If you want to serve Chicken Manchurian as a snack, reduce the quantity of chicken stock and cornstarch used in the sauce.*

BEST OF CHINESE COOKING

CHENGFU CHICKEN

INGREDIENTS

Chicken breasts (boneless) ... 300 gms	White pepper powder..........¼ tsp
Dry sherry (optional)......... 2 tbsps	Sugar......................................1 tsp
Garlic..........................2-3 cloves	Salt......................................to taste
Spinach............ 2 medium bunches	Chicken stock....................2 cups
Spring onion...............................1	Oil................. 2 tbsps+to deep fry
Cornstarch .... 4 tbsps	Sichuan peppers...................8-10
Soy sauce .... 1 tbsp	White vinegar.................... 1 tbsp
Oyster sauce .... 2 tbsps	Red chilli flakes...................1 tsp

METHOD OF PREPARATION

1 Wash, trim and cut the chicken breasts into one inch sized pieces. Marinate the chicken pieces in dry sherry for half an hour. Peel and finely chop garlic.

2 Wash, trim and finely shred spinach. Wash, trim and slice spring onion and reserve some sliced greens for garnish. Blend two tablespoons of cornstarch in half a cup of water. Mix soy sauce, oyster sauce, white pepper powder, sugar and salt to taste in chicken stock.

3 Add remaining cornstarch to the marinated chicken and mix well. Heat sufficient oil in a wok and deep fry chicken pieces for two minutes or until light brown in colour. Remove and drain onto an absorbent kitchen towel.

4 Heat one tablespoon of oil in a wok or a pan, add chopped garlic and stir fry briefly. Add sliced spring onion and continue to stir fry for a minute more.

5 Add shredded spinach and cook for two minutes on high heat, stirring and tossing continuously. Remove and arrange the cooked spinach on a serving platter and keep warm.

6 Heat remaining oil in a wok, add Sichuan peppers and immediately stir in the sauce and spice mix.

7 Add fried chicken pieces and cook for two to three minutes. Stir in the blended cornstarch, white vinegar and cook for a minute or until the sauce thickens and coats the chicken pieces.

8 Remove chicken onto the platter with the cooked spinach and sprinkle red chilli flakes. Serve hot, garnished with the reserved spring onion greens.

Note : *Refer page no.129 for the recipe of Chicken Stock.*

CHICKEN WITH WALNUTS

INGREDIENTS

Chicken breasts (boneless) ... 400 gms	Yellow capsicum ..... ½ medium sized
Egg 1	Celery .... 1 stalk
Cornstarch .... 6 tbsps	Button mushrooms 4-6
Salt .... to taste	Walnuts kernels .... 1 cup
Soy sauce .... 2 tbsps	Red chillies whole 2-3
Garlic .... 4-6 cloves	Oil .... 3 tbsps + to deep fry
Onion .... 1 medium sized	Sugar .... ½ tsp
Capsicum .... 1 medium sized	Ajinomoto .... ¼ tsp
Red capsicum .... ½ medium sized	Chicken stock .... 1½ cups

METHOD OF PREPARATION

1 Wash, trim and cut boneless chicken into one inch sized pieces. Mix egg, four tablespoons of cornstarch, salt to taste, one tablespoon of soy sauce into the chicken pieces. Leave aside for half an hour.

2 Peel and finely chop the garlic. Peel, wash and cut onion into one inch sized pieces and separate the layers. Wash, halve, deseed and cut capsicum into one inch sized pieces. Wash, deseed and cut red and yellow capsicum into one inch sized pieces.

3 Wash, trim and cut celery stalk into one inch sized pieces. Blend remaining cornstarch in one cup of water. Wash, trim and cut button mushrooms into quarters.

4 Boil walnut kernels in sufficient water for two minutes, drain and transfer onto an absorbent kitchen towel to dry out. Remove stem and break red chillies into two.

5 Heat sufficient oil in a wok and deep-fry marinated chicken for two to three minutes. Remove and drain onto an absorbent kitchen towel.

6 Heat three tablespoons of oil in a wok or a pan, add chopped garlic, broken dry red chillies and stir fry briefly. Add onion, celery, button mushrooms, walnut kernels and continue to stir fry for a couple of minutes.

7 Add remaining soy sauce, sugar, ajinomoto, chicken stock and salt to taste. Bring it to a boil and stir in blended cornstarch. Cook on medium heat for a minute or until the sauce starts to thicken, stirring continuously.

8 Add fried chicken pieces, capsicum pieces and continue to cook for a couple of minutes on high heat, tossing and turning continuously. Remove onto a warm platter and serve hot.

Note : *Refer page no.129 for the recipe of Chicken Stock.*

BEST OF CHINESE COOKING

76

CHICKEN IN LEMON SAUCE

INGREDIENTS

Chicken breasts (boneless)...... 4-5	Oil............... 2 tbsps + to deep fry
Lemon juice......................... 3 tbsps	White pepper powder .... ½ tsp
Salt .... to taste	Ajinomoto ....¼ tsp
Cornstarch .... 6 tbsps	Sugar.................................... 3 tbsps
Capsicum .... 1 small sized	Star anise.................................1
Red capsicum........... ½ small sized	Lemon rind (grated) .... 1 tsp
Yellow capsicum .....½ small sized	Chicken stock...................... 2 cups

METHOD OF PREPARATION

1 Trim, wash and drain chicken breasts. Marinate the chicken in one tablespoon of lemon juice and salt. Blend two tablespoons of cornstarch in half a cup of water.

2 Wash, halve, deseed and cut capsicum into one inch sized pieces. Wash, deseed and cut red and yellow capsicum into one inch sized triangles.

3 Heat sufficient oil in a wok, roll marinated chicken breasts in remaining cornstarch and deep fry for three to four minutes or until crisp and light golden brown. Drain onto an absorbent paper.

4 Heat two tablespoons of oil in a wok or a pan, add capsicum pieces and stir fry briefly.

5 Add white pepper powder, ajinomoto, sugar, salt to taste, star anise, lemon rind, chicken stock and bring it to a boil.

6 Stir in blended cornstarch and cook on medium heat for a minute or until the sauce starts to thicken. Add fried chicken breasts, reduce heat and simmer for a couple of minutes.

7 Stir in the remaining lemon juice and serve hot.

Note : *Refer page no.129 for the recipe of Chicken Stock.*

TWICE COOKED FIERY CHICKEN

INGREDIENTS

Whole chicken .... 1 kg	Fennel seeds .... 1 tbsp
Spring onion 1	Dark soy sauce .... ¼ cup
Green chillies 4	Sugar .... 2 tbsps
Dried orange peel .... 2 inch piece	Rice wine (optional) .... 2 tbsps
Celery .... 1 stalk	Salt .... to taste
Peppercorns .... 1 tbsp	Cornstarch .... 1 tbsp
Ginger .... 2 inch piece	Oil .... 4 tbsps
Cinnamon .... 1 inch stick	Ajinomoto .... ¼ tsp
Star anise 2	Sesame oil .... 1 tbsp

METHOD OF PREPARATION

1   Clean, wash and pat dry the chicken. Wash, trim and chop spring onion. Wash, remove stem and slice green chillies.

2   Roughly chop orange peel and celery, lightly crush peppercorns, ginger, cinnamon, star anise, fennel seeds and tie them into a bundle in a muslin cloth.

3   Take a deep pan, place the chicken and pour three litres of water. Add soy sauce, sugar, rice wine, one teaspoon salt and spice bundle. Stir the mixture and bring it to a boil.

4   Reduce heat and simmer for five to six minutes or until the chicken is almost cooked. Remove from heat and let the chicken marinate in this cooking liquor for at least three to four hours.

5   Remove the chicken and cut into ten to twelve pieces. Reserve one cup of cooking liquor in which chicken has been cooked and blend cornstarch in it.

6   Heat oil in a wok or a pan, add chicken pieces and stir fry for two to three minutes. Add spring onion, green chillies and continue to stir fry for another minute.

7   Stir in the blended cornstarch, cooking liquor, ajinomoto and cook on high heat for a minute, stirring continuously. Adjust seasoning, drizzle sesame oil and serve hot.

GARLIC CHICKEN

INGREDIENTS

Chicken (boneless) ....400 gms	Tomato ketchup ....½ cup
Garlic .... 18-20 cloves	Ajinomoto (optional) .... ¼ tsp
Spring onion greens.................. 2	Chicken stock .... 3 cups
Eggs 2	White pepper powder ...... ½ tsp
Cornstarch .... 6 tbsps	Oil .... 2 tbsps+to deep fry
Salt ....to taste	Vinegar................................. 1 tbsp

METHOD OF PREPARATION

1 Wash, trim and cut boneless chicken into one and half inch sized pieces. Peel and finely chop ten to twelve garlic cloves and grind the remaining into a fine paste. Wash, trim and chop spring onion greens.

2 Mix eggs, four tablespoons of cornstarch, garlic paste and salt to taste, into the chicken pieces. Leave aside for half an hour. Blend remaining cornstarch in one cup of water.

3 Blend tomato ketchup, ajinomoto, chicken stock, salt to taste and white pepper powder.

4 Heat sufficient oil in a wok and deep fry marinated chicken for two to three minutes. Remove and drain onto an absorbent kitchen towel.

5 Heat two tablespoons of oil in a wok or a pan, add chopped garlic and stir fry briefly.

6 Stir in sauce and spice mix and bring it to a boil. Stir in blended cornstarch and cook for a minute or until the sauce starts to thicken, stirring continuously.

7 Add fried chicken pieces and cook for a couple of minutes on medium heat. Stir in vinegar and serve hot, garnished with chopped spring onion greens.

Note : *Refer page no.129 for the recipe of Chicken Stock.*

Chef's Tip : *My colleague Chef Levy Yu Ping adds chopped garlic at the end to get a more pronounced garlic taste.*

CHICKEN WITH BROCCOLI AND PEPPERS

INGREDIENTS

Chicken (boneless)	400 gms	Ajinomoto	¼ tsp
Eggs	2	Rice wine (optional)	2 tbsps
Cornstarch	6 tbsps	Chicken stock	2 cups
Salt	to taste	White pepper powder	½ tsp
Soy sauce	2 tbsps	Cinnamon powder	¼ tsp
Garlic	2 cloves	Oyster sauce	1 tbsp
Capsicum	1 medium sized	Oil	4 tbsps + to deep fry
Broccoli	½ medium sized	Toasted sesame seeds	2 tsps

METHOD OF PREPARATION

1 Wash, trim and cut boneless chicken into one inch sized pieces. Mix eggs, four tablespoons of cornstarch, salt to taste, one tablespoon of soy sauce into the chicken pieces. Leave aside for half an hour.

2 Peel and finely chop the garlic. Wash, halve, deseed and cut capsicum into one inch sized triangular pieces. Wash, trim and cut broccoli into medium sized florets. Blend remaining cornstarch in one cup of water.

3 Blend remaining soy sauce, ajinomoto, rice wine, chicken stock, salt to taste, white pepper powder, cinnamon powder and oyster sauce.

4 Heat sufficient oil in a wok and deep fry marinated chicken for two to three minutes. Remove and drain onto an absorbent kitchen towel.

5 Heat four tablespoons of oil in a wok or a pan, add chopped garlic and stir fry briefly. Add broccoli florets and continue to stir fry for a couple of minutes.

6 Stir in sauce and spice mix and bring it to a boil. Stir in blended cornstarch and cook for a minute or until the sauce starts to thicken, stirring continuously.

7 Add fried chicken and capsicum pieces and cook for a couple of minutes on medium heat.

8 Sprinkle toasted sesame seeds and serve hot.

Note : *Refer page no.129 for the recipe of Chicken Stock.*

CHICKEN WITH CASHEWNUTS

INGREDIENTS

Chicken breasts (boneless) ... 400 gms	Oil .... 4 tbsps
Onion .... 1 medium sized	Cashewnuts .... ¾ cup
Capsicum .... 1 medium sized	White pepper powder .... ½ tsp
Garlic .... 10-12 cloves	Ajinomoto .... ¼ tsp
Cornstarch .... 3 tbsps	Salt .... to taste
Carrot .... 1 medium sized	Chicken stock .... 3 cups

METHOD OF PREPARATION

1 Cut chicken breasts into one inch sized cubes. Peel, wash, cut onion into quarters and separate the layers. Wash, halve, deseed and cut capsicum into one inch sized pieces.

2 Peel and chop garlic. Blend cornstarch in one cup of water. Wash, peel and cut carrot into thin slices.

3 Heat oil in a wok or a pan, add cashewnuts and stir fry briefly. Remove with a slotted spoon and drain onto an absorbent kitchen towel.

4 Add chopped garlic and stir fry briefly. Add chicken pieces, onion, sliced carrot and continue to stir fry for two to three minutes more.

5 Add white pepper powder, ajinomoto, salt to taste and stir in the chicken stock. Cook on high heat for two minutes, stirring continuously.

6 Stir in blended cornstarch, capsicum pieces and cook on medium heat for two to three minutes or until the sauce coats the chicken pieces. Add fried cashewnuts, mix well and serve hot.

Note : *Refer page no.129 for the recipe of Chicken Stock.*

Chicken With Cashewnuts (Page 85) & Spiced Shredded Chicken (Page 86)

SPICED SHREDDED CHICKEN

INGREDIENTS

Chicken (boneless)	400 gms	Garlic	3-4 cloves
Light soy sauce	1 tbsp	Green chillies	3-4
Dry sherry (optional)	1 tbsp	Oyster sauce	2 tbsps
Salt	to taste	Sugar	1 tsp
Onion	1 medium sized	Chilli sauce	3 tbsps
Capsicum	1 medium sized	Cornstarch	2 tbsps
Red capsicum	½ medium sized	Chicken stock	1 cup
Yellow capsicum	½ medium sized	Oil	4 tbsps
Ginger	1 inch piece	Peppercorns (crushed)	½ tsp

METHOD OF PREPARATION

1 Cut boneless chicken into thin strips. Mix chicken with light soy sauce, dry sherry and salt to taste. Leave aside to marinate for half an hour.

2 Peel, wash, halve and slice onion. Wash, halve, deseed and cut capsicum into strips. Wash, deseed and cut red and yellow capsicum into strips. Peel and finely chop the ginger and garlic.

3 Wash, remove stem and diagonally slice green chillies. Mix oyster sauce, sugar, chilli sauce and cornstarch in chicken stock.

4 Heat oil in a wok or a pan, add chopped ginger, garlic, green chillies and stir fry briefly. Add marinated chicken, sliced onion, capsicums and continue to stir fry for two to three minutes.

5 Stir in sauce and spice mix and cook on high heat for two minutes, tossing and stirring continuously.

6 Sprinkle crushed peppercorns and serve hot.

Note : *Refer page no.129 for the recipe of Chicken Stock.*

CHILLI CHICKEN

INGREDIENTS

Chicken (boneless) .... 400 gms	Green chillies 6-8
Eggs 2	Capsicums ....2 medium sized
Cornstarch ....6 tbsps	Oil............... 3 tbsps + to deep fry
Salt ....to taste	Ajinomoto.............................¼ tsp
Soy sauce .... 2 tbsps	Peppercorns (crushed) ..... ½ tsp
Chilli sauce ....2 tbsps	Chicken stock....................3 cups
Onions .... 2 medium sized	Vinegar................................2 tbsps
Garlic...........................8-10 cloves	

METHOD OF PREPARATION

1 Wash, trim and cut boneless chicken into finger sized pieces. Mix eggs, four tablespoons cornstarch, salt to taste, one table spoon each of soy sauce and chilli sauce into the chicken pieces. Leave aside for half an hour.

2 Blend remaining cornstarch in half a cup of water and keep aside.

3 Peel, wash onions, halve and cut into thick slices. Peel and finely chop garlic. Wash, remove stem and slice green chillies. Wash, halve, deseed and cut capsicums into thick strips.

4 Heat sufficient oil in a wok and deep fry marinated chicken pieces for two minutes. Remove and drain onto an absorbent kitchen towel.

5 Heat three tablespoons of oil in a wok or a pan, add chopped garlic and stir fry briefly. Add onion and sliced green chillies. Continue to stir fry for a couple of minutes.

6 Add remaining soy sauce and chilli sauce, ajinomoto, crushed peppercorns, salt to taste and stir in the chicken stock. Bring it to a boil and stir in blended cornstarch.

7 Cook on high heat for a minute or until the sauce starts to thicken. Add fried chicken pieces, capsicums, vinegar and cook for a minute on high heat, stirring continuously and serve hot.

Note : *Refer page no.129 for the recipe of Chicken Stock.*

HONEY GLAZED CHICKEN

INGREDIENTS

Chicken (boneless) .... 400 gms	White pepper powder .... ½ tsp
Oil .... 3 tbsps + to deep fry	Salt .... to taste
Garlic .... 2-3 cloves	Chicken stock .... 1 ½ cups
Spring onion greens 2	Red chilli flakes .... 1 tbsp
Cornstarch .... 1½ tbsps	Honey .... 4 tbsps
Soy sauce .... 1 tbsp	Toasted sesame seeds ..... 1 tbsp
Ajinomoto .... ¼ tsp	

METHOD OF PREPARATION

1 Clean and cut chicken into one inch sized pieces. Heat sufficient oil in a wok and deep fry the chicken pieces on high heat for half a minute. Remove and drain onto an absorbent kitchen towel.

2 Peel and finely chop garlic. Wash, trim and chop spring onion greens. Blend cornstarch, soy sauce, ajinomoto, white pepper powder and salt to taste in chicken stock.

3 Heat three tablespoons of oil in a wok or a pan, add chopped garlic, red chilli flakes and stir fry briefly. Stir in the blended sauce and spice mix. Cook for a minute or until the sauce starts to thicken, stirring continuously.

4 Add fried chicken, stir in honey and cook for a minute, stirring and tossing continuously. Sprinkle toasted sesame seeds and serve hot, garnished with chopped spring onion greens.

Note : *Refer page no.129 for the recipe of Chicken Stock.*

STUFFED CHICKEN WITH PLUM SAUCE

INGREDIENTS

Chicken breasts (boneless)	4	Oil	6 tbsps
Spring onions	2	Chicken stock	1 ½ cups
Garlic	2-3 cloves	Plum sauce	½ cup
Green chillies	2	Ajinomoto	¼ tsp
Cornstarch	4 tbsps	White pepper powder	½ tsp
Salt	to taste	Five spice powder	¼ tsp
Lemon juice	2 tbsps	Chilli oil	2 tbsps
Chicken mince	100 gms		

METHOD OF PREPARATION

1   Clean, wash, pat dry and flatten the chicken breasts with a steak hammer or blunt side of a large knife. Wash, trim, finely chop spring onions and reserve the chopped greens for garnish.

2   Peel and chop garlic. Wash, remove stem and chop green chillies. Blend one tablespoon of cornstarch in half a cup of water.

3   Mix chopped spring onions, green chillies, chopped garlic, salt to taste and one tablespoon lemon juice with chicken mince. Divide it into four equal portions. Place a portion of chicken mince on one end of the flattened chicken breast, roll and secure the ends with tooth picks.

4   Heat oil in a wok or a pan, roll stuffed chicken breasts in remaining cornstarch and shallow fry on medium heat for two minutes, turning occasionally. Add half a cup of chicken stock and continue to cook for another two to three minutes. Remove cooked chicken breasts and keep warm.

5   Reheat wok or the pan in which chicken breasts were cooked, stir in the remaining stock, plum sauce, ajinomoto, white pepper powder, five spice powder and salt to taste. Bring it to a boil and stir in blended cornstarch and remaining lemon juice. Cook for a minute or until the sauce thickens, stirring continuously. Add chilli oil and mix.

6   Meanwhile remove toothpicks from chicken breasts, slice each breast into two to three pieces and arrange in a platter or a shallow serving dish.

7   Pour the plum sauce on top of the sliced chicken breasts. Serve hot, garnished with chopped spring onion greens.

Note : *Refer page no.129 for the recipe of Chicken Stock.*

KUNG PAO CHICKEN

INGREDIENTS

Chicken breasts (boneless) .... 400 gms	Ginger .... 1 inch piece
Eggs 2	Garlic .... 4-5 cloves
Cornstarch .... 6 tbsps	Oil.............. 4 tbsps + to deep fry
Lemon juice..................... 1½ tbsps	Soy sauce .... 2 tbsps
White pepper powder .... ½ tsp	Sugar.................................. 2 tsps
Ajinomoto .... ¼ tsp	Rice wine (optional) .... 3 tbsps
Salt .... to taste	Chicken stock....................½ cup
Red chillies whole 5-6	Roasted peanuts .... ¼ cup
Spring onions 2	Chilli oil .... 2 tbsps

METHOD OF PREPARATION

1 Cut chicken breasts into one inch sized cubes. Mix eggs, four tablespoons of cornstarch, lemon juice, white pepper powder, ajinomoto and salt into the chicken pieces. Leave aside to marinate for half an hour.

2 Remove stem and break red chillies into two. Blend remaining cornstarch in half a cup of water.

3 Wash, trim and finely chop the spring onions and keep some chopped spring onion greens aside for garnish. Wash, peel and finely chop ginger and garlic.

4 Heat sufficient oil in a wok and deep fry the marinated chicken for three minutes or until the chicken is light golden brown in colour. Remove and drain onto an absorbent kitchen towel.

5 Heat four tablespoons of oil in a wok or a pan, add broken red chillies, chopped ginger, garlic and stir fry briefly. Add chopped spring onions and continue to stir fry for a minute more.

6 Add soy sauce, sugar, rice wine and salt to taste. Stir in the chicken stock and cook briefly. Stir in blended cornstarch and immediately add fried chicken and peanuts. Cook for two minutes on high heat, stirring continuously.

7 Drizzle chilli oil and serve hot, garnished with reserved chopped spring onion greens.

Note : *Refer page no.129 for the recipe of Chicken Stock.*

Chef's Tip : *You can substitute the peanuts with roasted cashewnuts or even almonds, if you like.*

THREE PEPPER CHICKEN

INGREDIENTS

Chicken (boneless)	400 gms	Sugar	1 tsp
Spring onions	2	Soy sauce	1 ½ tbsps
Ginger	1 inch piece	Ajinomoto	¼ tsp
Garlic	4-5 cloves	Salt	to taste
Capsicum	1 medium sized	Chicken stock	2 cups
Sichuan peppers	8-10	Vinegar	1 tbsp
Cornstarch	3 tbsps	Peppercorns (crushed)	2 tsps
Oil	4 tbsps		

METHOD OF PREPARATION

1 Cut chicken into one inch sized pieces. Wash, trim, chop spring onions and reserve some chopped greens for garnish. Peel and finely chop ginger and garlic.

2 Wash, halve, deseed and cut capsicum into one inch sized pieces. Dry roast Sichuan peppers and crush lightly. Blend cornstarch in one cup of water.

3 Heat oil in a wok or a pan, add chopped ginger, garlic and stir fry briefly. Add chopped spring onions and continue to stir fry for a couple of minutes.

4 Add chicken pieces and cook for two to three minutes, stirring continuously. Add sugar, soy sauce, ajinomoto, capsicum, salt to taste and stir in chicken stock.

5 Bring it to a boil and cook the chicken for two minutes. Stir in blended cornstarch, Sichuan peppers and cook for two to three minutes or until the sauce coats the chicken pieces.

6 Stir in vinegar, crushed pepper corns and serve hot, garnished with chopped spring onion greens.

Note : *Refer page no.129 for the recipe of Chicken Stock.*

CHICKEN IN A NEST

INGREDIENTS

Chicken breasts (boneless) ... 300 gms	White pepper powder ....½ tsp
Ginger ....1 inch piece	Red chilli sauce .... 2 tbsps
Garlic ....2-3 cloves	Sugar... 1 tsp
Spring onion greens 2	Salt.....................................to taste
Cornstarch .... 4 tbsps + ½ cup	Potatoes .... 4-5 medium sized
Soy sauce ....1½ tbsps	Oil.................2 tbsps+to deep fry
Chicken stock ....1½ cups	Honey......................................2 tbsps
Egg.. 1	Toasted sesame seeds ....1 tbsp

METHOD OF PREPARATION

1   Wash, trim and cut chicken into one inch sized pieces. Peel and finely chop ginger and garlic. Wash, trim and finely slice spring onion greens. Blend two tablespoons of cornstarch and soy sauce in the chicken stock.

2   Mix chicken with egg, two tablespoons of cornstarch, white pepper powder, red chilli sauce, sugar and salt to taste. Leave aside the chicken mixture for an hour to marinate, preferably in a refrigerator.

3   Wash and peel potatoes. Using a vegetable grater, grate them into thick shreds. Immediately mix half a cup of cornstarch into the grated potatoes. Line a six inch diameter wire sieve with a quarter portion of the potato mixture and press another sieve of the same size on top.

4   Heat sufficient oil in a wok and lower the sieves into the oil and fry for two to three minutes or until the potato nest is golden brown and crisp. Remove from the wok allowing the excess oil to drain off. Transfer to an absorbent kitchen towel. Similarly make three more baskets with the remaining potato mixture.

5   Reheat the oil and deep fry the marinated chicken for three to four minutes or until golden brown in colour. Remove and drain onto an absorbent kitchen towel.

6   Heat two tablespoons of oil in a wok or a pan, add chopped ginger, garlic and stir fry briefly. Stir in the blended cornstarch mixture and cook for a minute more or until the sauce starts to thicken.

7   Add fried chicken, honey and stir well to coat. Transfer the chicken into the crisp potato nests. Sprinkle toasted sesame seeds and serve hot, garnished with sliced spring onion greens.

Note : *Refer page no.129 for the recipe of Chicken Stock.*

BEST OF CHINESE COOKING

Salt and Pepper Crispy Lamb (Page 96) ▶

SIZZLING GINGER CHICKEN

INGREDIENTS

Chicken (boneless) .... 400 gms
Ginger .... four 1 inch pieces
Spring onions 2
Capsicum .... 1 medium sized
Mushrooms 4-6
Babycorns 3-4
Red chillies whole 3-4

Oil .... 4 tbsps
Soy sauce .... 2 tbsps
Salt .... to taste
Ajinomoto .... ¼ tsp
Peppercorns (crushed) .... ½ tsp
Chicken stock .... ½ cup
Bean sprouts .... ½ cup

METHOD OF PREPARATION

1   Clean and cut chicken into thin strips. Wash, peel and cut ginger into julienne. Wash, trim, slice spring onion and reserve sliced greens for garnish.

2   Wash, halve, deseed and cut capsicum into julienne. Clean, wash and thinly slice mushrooms. Trim, wash and diagonally slice each babycorn into three to four pieces. Remove stem and break red chillies into two.

3   Heat oil in a wok, add broken red chillies, ginger julienne and stir fry briefly. Add chicken strips and continue to stir fry for another minute.

4   Add sliced spring onions, babycorns, mushrooms, soy sauce, salt, ajinomoto and crushed peppercorn. Stir fry for half a minute and stir in chicken stock. Add capsicum julienne and cook on high heat for two to three minutes, stirring and tossing continuously.

5   Add bean sprouts, mix well and serve hot garnished with reserved sliced spring onion greens.

6   Alternatively heat a cast iron sizzler plate on direct fire of the gas burner till the plate is almost red hot. Transfer the hot sizzler plate onto its wooden base carefully and immediately place the prepared ginger chicken. Serve sizzling, garnished with reserved sliced spring onion greens.

Note : *Refer page no.129 for the recipe of Chicken Stock.*

BEST OF CHINESE COOKING

95

◀ *Quick Fried Prawns With Mushrooms (Page 98)*

SALT AND PEPPER CRISPY LAMB

INGREDIENTS

Mutton (boneless) .... 400 gms	Oil.................................. to deep fry
Ginger .... 1 inch piece	Chilli oil .... 4 tbsps
Garlic .... 4-6 cloves	Soy sauce .... 1 tbsp
Celery .... ½ stalk	Peppercorns (crushed) .... 1 tsp
Spring onion 1	Sugar.................................... 2 tsps
Red chillies whole 5-6	Ajinomoto ....¼ tsp
Cornstarch .... 4 tbsps	Salt ....to taste

METHOD OF PREPARATION

1 Clean and cut mutton into very thin strips. Wash, peel and finely chop ginger. Peel and finely chop garlic. Wash, trim and finely chop celery.

2 Wash, trim and chop spring onion. Diagonally slice spring onion greens and reserve for garnish. Remove stem and break red chillies into two.

3 Mix cornstarch thoroughly into mutton pieces. Heat sufficient oil in a wok and deep fry cornstarch coated mutton pieces for four to five minutes or until crisp. Remove and drain onto an absorbent kitchen towel.

4 Heat chilli oil in a wok or a pan, add broken red chillies, chopped ginger, garlic, celery and stir fry briefly. Add chopped spring onion and continue to stir fry for a minute more.

5 Add fried mutton pieces, soy sauce, crushed peppercorns, sugar, ajinomoto and salt to taste. Cook on high heat for a minute, tossing continuously.

6 Serve hot, garnished with sliced spring onion greens.

Chef's Tip : *The secret of this recipe lies in retaining the crispness of the mutton pieces by frying till they are very crisp.*

SLICED LAMB WITH GREEN PEPPERS

INGREDIENTS

Mutton (boneless)	400 gms	Green chillies	3-4
Soy sauce	2 tbsps	Capsicum	1 medium sized
Red wine	½ cup	Cornstarch	2 tbsps
Peppercorns (crushed)	½ tsp	Oil	4 tbsps
Salt	to taste	Ajinomoto	¼ tsp
Spring onions	2	Sugar	1 tsp
Ginger	1 inch piece	Chicken stock	2 cups
Garlic	4-6 cloves		

METHOD OF PREPARATION

1. Clean and slice mutton into thin slices. Mix one tablespoon of soy sauce, red wine, crushed peppercorns and half a teaspoon of salt with sliced mutton. Leave the mutton to marinate for atleast an hour.

2. Wash, trim, chop spring onions and reserve chopped greens for garnish. Wash, peel and grate ginger. Peel and crush garlic. Wash, remove stem and slice green chillies.

3. Wash, halve, deseed and cut capsicum into julienne. Blend cornstarch in one cup of water.

4. Heat oil in a wok or a pan, add crushed garlic, grated ginger, sliced green chillies, chopped spring onions and stir fry briefly. Add marinated mutton and continue to cook on high heat for two to three minutes, stirring continuously.

5. Add remaining soy sauce, ajinomoto, sugar and salt to taste. Stir in the chicken stock and bring it to a boil. Reduce heat and simmer for ten to twelve minutes or until mutton is cooked.

6. Stir in blended cornstarch, capsicum julienne and cook for two to three minutes or until the sauce thickens. Serve hot, garnished with reserved chopped spring onion greens.

Note : *Refer page no.129 for the recipe of Chicken Stock.*

Chef's Tip : *Cooking time of mutton may vary depending upon the quality of the meat. To reduce the cooking time you may precook mutton by boiling or roasting. Slicing of meat becomes relatively easy if you keep the meat in the freezer for an hour before cutting.*

QUICK FRIED PRAWNS WITH MUSHROOMS

INGREDIENTS

Whole prawns	16 medium sized	Cornstarch	2 tbsps
Oyster mushrooms	4-6	Fish or chicken stock	2 cups
Chinese mushrooms (dried)	4-6	Soy sauce	2 tbsps
Mushrooms	6-8	Oyster sauce	1 tbsp
Capsicum	1 medium sized	Salt	to taste
Yellow capsicum	½ medium sized	Ajinomoto	¼ tsp
Garlic	2-3 cloves	Peppercorns (crushed)	1 tsp
Ginger	1 inch piece	Oil	4 tbsps
Spring onions	2	Malt vinegar	1 tbsp

METHOD OF PREPARATION

1. Wash and shell the prawns, keeping head and tip of the tail intact. Devein, wash them thoroughly and pat dry with an absorbent kitchen towel. Soak oyster mushrooms and Chinese mushrooms in sufficient hot water for fifteen minutes. Drain, wash and slice them.

2. Clean, wash, trim and slice mushrooms. Wash, halve, deseed and cut capsicum into thick strips. Wash, deseed and cut yellow capsicum into thick strips.

3. Peel and finely chop garlic. Wash, peel and thinly slice ginger. Wash, trim and diagonally slice spring onions. Blend cornstarch in one cup of stock. Mix soy sauce, oyster sauce, salt to taste, ajinomoto and crushed peppercorns in the remaining stock.

4. Heat oil in a wok or a pan, add chopped garlic and stir fry briefly. Add sliced spring onions, sliced ginger, prawns, capsicums and mushrooms. Continue to stir fry for two minutes, tossing continuously.

5. Stir in prepared sauce and spice mix. Cook on high heat for half a minute. Add blended cornstarch and continue to cook for a minute or until the sauce thickens, stirring continuously.

6. Stir in malt vinegar and serve hot.

Note : *Refer page no.131 for the recipe of Fish Stock or page no. 129 for the recipe of Chicken Stock.*

CHILLI GARLIC CRAB

INGREDIENTS

Crabs .... 2 large sized	Sugar .... 1 tsp
Garlic .... 14-16 cloves	Ajinomoto ....¼ tsp
Red chillies whole 3-4	Fish or chicken stock ...... 1 ½ cups
Cornstarch .... 2 tbsps	Peppercorns (crushed) .... ½ tsp
Spring onion greens 2	Salt ....to taste
Oil .... 4 tbsps	Dry sherry (optional) ....2 tbsps
Red chilli paste .... 2 tbsps	Vinegar .... 1 tbsp
Soy sauce .... 1 tbsp	Sesame oil .... 2 tbsps

METHOD OF PREPARATION

1   Separate the claws and cut the crab into four pieces. Wash and remove gills and stomach sac from underside. Crack the claws lightly, wash thoroughly and drain well.

2   Peel and crush garlic. Remove stem and break red chillies into two. Blend cornstarch in half a cup of water. Wash, trim and chop the spring onion greens.

3   Heat oil in a wok or a pan, add crushed garlic, broken red chillies and stir fry briefly. Add red chilli paste, soy sauce, sugar, ajinomoto and immediately add the crab pieces. Continue to stir fry for two to three minutes, stirring continuously.

4   Stir in the stock and cook for two minutes or until the crabs are cooked. Stir in blended cornstarch and cook for a minute or until the sauce starts to thicken. Add crushed peppercorns, salt to taste and stir in dry sherry and vinegar.

5   Drizzle sesame oil and serve hot, garnished with chopped spring onion greens.

Note : *Refer page no.131 for the recipe of Fish Stock or page no. 129 for the recipe of Chicken Stock.*

Chef's Tip : *Ensure that you buy fresh crabs and preferably have them cut by your fishmonger as it can be quite messy to cut crabs in your kitchen.*

FISH IN HOT BEAN SAUCE

INGREDIENTS

Fish fillets	400 gms	Oyster sauce	2 tbsps
Cornstarch	6 tbsps	Hot black bean paste	2 tbsps
Oil	4 tbsps + to deep fry	Sugar	1 tsp
Onion	1 medium sized	Salt	to taste
Ginger	1 inch piece	Fish or chicken stock	2 cups
Green chillies	3-4	Malt vinegar	1 tbsp
Coriander leaves	½ cup	Peppercorns (crushed)	1 tsp

METHOD OF PREPARATION

1   Wash, pat dry and cut fish fillets into one and half inch sized pieces. Roll the fish pieces in three tablespoons of cornstarch. Heat sufficient oil in a wok, add cornstarch coated fish pieces and deep fry for a minute. Remove and drain onto an absorbent kitchen towel.

2   Peel, wash and finely slice onion. Wash, peel and grate ginger. Wash, remove stem and slice green chillies. Wash, trim and finely chop coriander leaves.

3   Blend the remaining cornstarch in one cup of water. Mix oyster sauce, hot black bean paste, sugar, salt to taste in one cup of stock.

4   Heat four tablespoons of oil in a wok or a pan, add grated ginger, sliced onion, green chillies and stir fry for a minute, stirring continuously. Stir in the sauce and spice mix, remaining stock and bring to a boil.

5   Stir in blended cornstarch and cook for a minute or until the sauce starts to thicken. Add fried fish pieces and cook for a minute more, stirring gently.

6   Stir in malt vinegar, crushed peppercorns and serve hot, garnished with chopped coriander leaves.

Note : *Refer page no.131 for the recipe of Fish Stock or page no. 129 for the recipe of Chicken Stock.*

CANTONESE FISH

INGREDIENTS

Fish fillets	400 gms	Soy sauce	2 tbsps
Cornstarch	3 tbsps	Ajinomoto	¼ tsp
Oil	3 tbsps + to deep fry	White pepper powder	½ tsp
Spring onions	2	Sugar	½ tsp
Celery	1 stalk	Salt	to taste
Carrot	1 medium sized	White wine	½ cup
Ginger	2 inch piece	Chicken stock	1½ cups
Bamboo shoot	1 slice		

METHOD OF PREPARATION

1   Wash, pat dry and cut fish fillets into one and half inch sized pieces. Roll the fish pieces in three tablespoons of cornstarch. Heat sufficient oil in a wok, add cornstarch coated fish pieces and deep fry for a minute. Remove and drain onto an absorbent kitchen towel.

2   Wash, trim and thinly slice spring onions and celery. Wash, peel and thinly slice carrot. Wash, peel and thinly slice ginger.

3   Soak the bamboo shoot in one cup of hot water for ten minutes. Drain and slice.

4   Heat oil in a wok or a pan, add sliced ginger, celery, spring onions and stir fry briefly. Add carrot, bamboo shoot and continue to stir fry for half a minute.

5   Add soy sauce, ajinomoto, white pepper powder, sugar, salt to taste, white wine and stir in the stock. Bring it to a boil, reduce heat and simmer for three to four minutes.

6   Gently slide in the fried fish pieces and continue to simmer for a minute, without stirring and serve hot.

Note : *Refer page no.129 for the recipe of Chicken Stock.*

WHOLE POMFRET - MANDARIN STYLE

INGREDIENTS

Pomfrets	2 medium sized	Cornstarch .... 1 tbsp
Salt	to taste	Tomato sauce .... ¼ cup
Lemon juice	2 tbsps	Ajinomoto .... ¼ tsp
Chilli oil	1 tbsp	White pepper powder .... ¼ tsp
Spring onion greens	1	Red chilli flakes .... 1 tbsp
Garlic	3-4 cloves	Sugar.................................... 2 tbsps
Capsicum	½ medium sized	Chicken stock....................... 1 cup
Pineapple slice	1	Oil............... 2 tbsps + to deep fry
Coriander leaves	a few sprigs	

METHOD OF PREPARATION

1 Make a small slit at the stomach and clean the inside of the pomfret. Wash the fish thoroughly and pat dry with an absorbent kitchen towel.

2 Make four to five quarter inch deep cuts on both sides of the fish, apply salt, lemon juice and chilli oil. Leave aside to marinate for half an hour.

3 Wash, trim and chop spring onion greens. Peel and chop garlic. Wash, deseed and cut capsicum into half inch sized pieces. Cut pineapple slice into half inch sized pieces. Wash, trim and keep coriander sprigs in chilled water. Blend cornstarch in half a cup of water.

4 Mix tomato sauce, ajinomoto, white pepper powder, chilli flakes, sugar and salt to taste with chicken stock.

5 Heat sufficient oil in a wok and deep fry marinated pomfret for two to three minutes. Remove and drain onto an absorbent kitchen towel. Keep warm in a serving platter.

6 Heat oil in a wok or a pan, add chopped garlic and capsicum and stir fry briefly.

7 Stir in the prepared sauce and spice mix. Bring it to a boil, add pineapple and blended cornstarch. Continue to cook on high heat for a minute.

8 Pour the sauce on the fried pomfret. Remove coriander sprigs from water and garnish the pomfret. Serve hot topped with spring onion greens.

Note : *Refer page no.129 for the recipe of Chicken Stock.*

BEST OF CHINESE COOKING

102

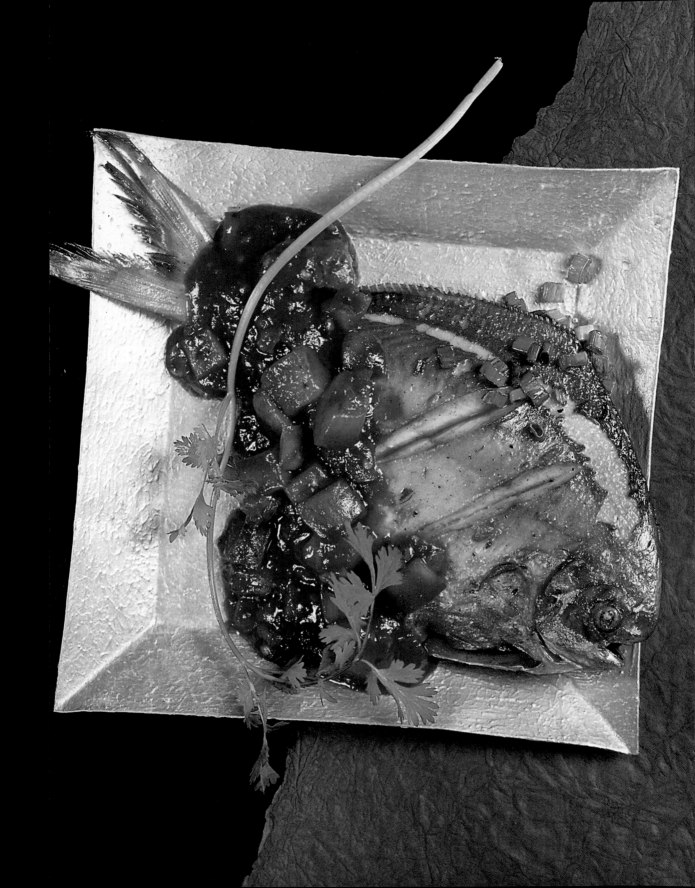

FRIED CHILLI PRAWNS

INGREDIENTS

Prawns (shelled) .... 16 medium sized	Green chillies 4-6
Lemon juice .... 2 tbsps	Ginger .... 2 inch piece
Chilli sauce .... 1 tbsp	Garlic .... 6-8 cloves
Salt .... to taste	Soy sauce .... 2 tbsps
Cornstarch .... 6 tbsps	White pepper powder .... ½ tsp
Oil .... 4 tbsps + to deep fry	Ajinomoto .... ¼ tsp
Spring onions 2	Sugar .... 1 tsp
Capsicum .... 1 medium sized	Fish or chicken stock .... 1 cup

METHOD OF PREPARATION

1 Clean, devein, wash and pat dry prawns thoroughly with an absorbent kitchen towel. Mix one tablespoon of lemon juice, chilli sauce, salt to taste with the prawns.

2 Roll the prawns in four tablespoons of cornstarch. Heat sufficient oil in a wok, add cornstarch coated prawns and deep fry for a minute. Do not overcook. Remove and drain onto an absorbent kitchen towel.

3 Wash, trim, chop spring onions and reserve some greens for garnish. Wash, halve, deseed and cut capsicum into strips. Wash, remove stem and diagonally slice green chillies. Peel and finely chop ginger and garlic. Blend remaining cornstarch in half a cup of water.

4 Heat four tablespoons of oil a wok or a pan, add chopped ginger, garlic, sliced green chillies and stir fry briefly. Add chopped spring onions and continue to stir fry for a couple of minutes more.

5 Add soy sauce, white pepper powder, ajinomoto, sugar, salt to taste and immediately stir in the stock. Add fried prawns, capsicum strips and stir fry for a couple of minutes, stirring continuously.

6 Stir in blended cornstarch and cook for a minute more or until the sauce coats the prawns. Stir in remaining lemon juice and serve hot, garnished with chopped spring onion greens.

Note : *Refer page no.131 for the recipe of Fish Stock or page no. 129 for the recipe of Chicken Stock.*

Chef's Tip : *If you are using large prawns, leave tip of the tail on for better presentation.*

105

MONGOLIAN PRAWNS

INGREDIENTS

Prawns (shelled) ... 16 medium sized	Tomato sauce .... 4 tbsps
Cornstarch .... 6 tbsps	White pepper powder .... ½ tsp
Oil .... 4 tbsps + to deep fry	Ajinomoto .... ¼ tsp
Spring onions 2	Sugar .... 2 tsps
Red chillies whole 3-4	Salt .... to taste
Ginger .... 1 inch piece	Fish or chicken stock .... 2 cups
Garlic .... 4-6 cloves	Malt vinegar .... 1 tbsp
Red chilli paste .... 2 tbsps	

METHOD OF PREPARATION

1   Clean, devein, wash and pat dry prawns thoroughly with an absorbent kitchen towel. Roll the prawns in three tablespoons of cornstarch. Heat sufficient oil in a wok, add cornstarch coated prawns and deep fry for a minute. Remove and drain onto an absorbent kitchen towel.

2   Wash, trim, halve, slice spring onions and reserve the greens for garnish. Remove stem and break red chillies into two. Peel and finely chop ginger and garlic. Blend remaining cornstarch in half a cup of water. Mix red chilli paste, tomato sauce, white pepper powder, ajinomoto, sugar and salt to taste in one cup of stock.

3   Heat four tablespoons of oil a wok or a pan, add broken red chillies, chopped ginger, garlic and stir fry briefly. Add sliced spring onion and continue to stir fry for a couple of minutes more.

4   Add the sauce and spice mix, remaining stock and bring it to a boil. Stir in blended cornstarch and cook for a minute or until the sauce starts to thicken.

5   Add fried prawns and cook for two minutes, or until the sauce coats the prawns, stirring and tossing continuously. Stir in malt vinegar and serve hot, garnished with chopped spring onion greens.

Note : *Refer page no.131 for the recipe of Fish Stock or page no. 129 for the recipe of Chicken Stock.*

INGREDIENTS

Prawns (shelled) .... 16 medium sized	Soy sauce .... 1 tbsp
Spring onions 2	Rice wine (optional) .... ¼ cup
Red chillies whole 3-4	Ajinomoto ....¼ tsp
Ginger .... 1 inch piece	Sugar....................................... 2 tsps
Garlic............................ 6-8 cloves	Salt....................................... to taste
Capsicum .... 1 medium sized	Fish or chicken stock ..... 2 cups
Cornstarch .... 3 tbsps	Oil....................................... 6 tbsps
Red chilli paste .... 2 tbsps	Sichuan peppers 6-8
Tomato sauce .... 3 tbsps	Vinegar................................ 1 tbsp

METHOD OF PREPARATION

1 Clean, devein, wash and pat dry prawns thoroughly with an absorbent kitchen towel.

2 Wash, trim, chop spring onions and reserve the greens for garnish. Remove stem and break red chillies into two. Peel and finely chop ginger and garlic. Wash, halve, deseed and cut capsicum into one inch sized pieces.

3 Blend cornstarch in one cup of water. Mix red chilli paste, tomato sauce, soy sauce, rice wine, ajinomoto, sugar and salt to taste in one cup of stock.

4 Heat four tablespoons of oil a wok or a pan, add broken red chillies, Sichuan peppers, chopped ginger, garlic and stir fry briefly. Add chopped spring onions and continue to stir fry for a minute more.

5 Add prawns and cook for a minute or until the prawns turn white, stirring and tossing continuously. Add the sauce and spice mix, remaining stock and bring it to a boil.

6 Stir in blended cornstarch, add capsicum pieces and cook for two to three minutes or until the sauce coats the prawns. Stir in vinegar and serve hot, garnished with chopped spring onion greens.

Note : *Refer page no.131 for the recipe of Fish Stock or page no. 129 for the recipe of Chicken Stock.*

PEPPER GARLIC LOBSTER

INGREDIENTS

Lobsters	4 medium sized	Oil	1 tbsp
Lemon juice	3 tbsps	Butter	4 tbsps
Salt	to taste	Sugar	1 tsp
Coriander leaves	6-8 sprigs	Peppercorns (crushed)	½ tbsp
Onion	1 small sized	Chicken stock	2 cups
Garlic	14-16 cloves	Ajinomoto	¼ tsp
Cornstarch	2 tbsps		

METHOD OF PREPARATION

1 Remove head and shell from the lobster. Wash, pat dry with an absorbent kitchen towel and cut lobster into one inch sized pieces.

2 Add lemon juice, half teaspoon of salt into lobster pieces and leave aside to marinate for about half an hour.

3 Wash, trim and keep coriander sprigs in chilled water. Peel, wash and chop onion and garlic. Blend cornstarch in half a cup of water.

4 Heat oil and butter together in a wok or a pan. Add chopped onion, garlic and stir fry briefly. Add marinated lobsters, sugar and crushed peppercorns. Continue to stir fry for one minute.

5 Stir in chicken stock and bring to a boil. Add salt to taste, ajinomoto and stir in blended cornstarch. Cook on high heat for a minute or until sauce thickens and coats the lobster pieces.

6 Remove coriander sprigs from water and garnish the lobster.

Note : *Refer page no.129 for the recipe of Chicken Stock.*

Chef's Tip : *For better presentation use cooked lobster shells to serve this dish.*

SWEET AND SOUR FISH

INGREDIENTS

Fish fillets .... 400 gms	Pineapple slice 1
Oil ....3 tbsps+to deep fry	Tomato sauce .... 4 tbsps
Cornstarch .... 5 tbsps	Sugar..................................... 2 tbsps
Onion .... 1 medium sized	Pineapple juice ....½ cup
Ginger........................ 1 inch piece	Ajinomoto .... ¼ tsp
Garlic ....4-6 cloves	White pepper powder .... ½ tsp
Capsicum .... 1 medium sized	Salt....................................to taste
Red capsicum ...... ½ medium sized	Fish or chicken stock......... 2 cups
Yellow capsicum ....½ medium sized	Vinegar .... 2 tbsps

METHOD OF PREPARATION

1   Wash, pat dry fish fillets with an absorbent kitchen towel. Cut it into one inch sized pieces.

2   Heat sufficient oil in a wok, roll the fish pieces in two tablespoons of cornstarch and deep fry on medium heat until the edges start to turn brown. Remove and drain onto an absorbent kitchen towel.

3   Peel, wash onion, cut it into quarters and separate the layers. Peel and finely chop ginger and garlic. Wash, halve, deseed and cut capsicum into one inch sized pieces.

4   Wash, deseed and cut red and yellow capsicum into one inch sized pieces. Cut pineapple slice into one inch sized pieces. Blend the remaining cornstarch in one cup of water.

5   Blend tomato sauce, sugar, pineapple juice, ajinomoto, white pepper powder and salt to taste in one cup of stock.

6   Heat three tablespoons of oil in a wok or a pan, add chopped ginger, garlic and stir fry briefly. Add onion and continue to stir fry for a minute.

7   Stir in sauce and spice mix, capsicum pieces, remaining stock and blended cornstarch. Cook for a couple of minutes or until the sauce starts to thicken, stirring continuously.

8   Add fried fish, pineapple pieces and cook for a minute or until the sauce coats the fish pieces. Stir in vinegar and serve hot.

Note : *Refer page no.131 for the recipe of Fish Stock or page no. 129 for the recipe of Chicken Stock.*

SEAFOOD AND NOODLE STIR FRY

INGREDIENTS

Fish fillets .... 100 gms	Spring onion greens 1
Mussels or clams 6-8	Oil ....6 tbsps
Prawns (shelled) ..... 12 small sized	Soy sauce ....1 tbsp
Crabs .... 2 medium sized	Oyster sauce ....1 tbsp
Flat noodles .... 300 gms	White pepper powder ....½ tsp
Onion................. 1 medium sized	Ajinomoto ....¼ tsp
Capsicum .... 1 medium sized	Salt.......................................to taste
Garlic.............................6-8 cloves	Lemon juice ....1 tbsp
Ginger .... 1 inch piece	

METHOD OF PREPARATION

1   Wash and cut fish fillets into one inch sized pieces. Open mussels or clams shells with a knife and scoop the meat. Devein, wash thoroughly and pat dry prawns with an absorbent kitchen towel.

2   Boil crabs in sufficient water for three to four minutes. Cool, separate the claws, crack them lightly and keep aside. Remove meat from rest of the crab.

3   Boil flat noodles in sufficient water. Drain, remove and cool. Peel, wash, halve and slice onion. Wash, halve, deseed and cut capsicum into julienne. Peel and finely chop garlic. Wash, peel and finely chop ginger. Wash, trim and finely shred spring onion greens.

4   Heat oil in a wok, add chopped garlic, ginger, sliced onion and stir fry briefly. Add prawns, fish and mussels or clams, capsicum and continue to stir fry for a minute.

5   Add boiled flat noodles, crab meat, crab claws, soy sauce, oyster sauce, white pepper powder, ajinomoto, salt to taste and cook on high heat for a couple of minutes, tossing continuously.

6   Mix in lemon juice and serve hot, garnished with spring onion greens.

POT MUSHROOM RICE

INGREDIENTS

Rice	1 cup	Spring onions	2
Star anise	1	Oil	4 tbsps
Oyster mushrooms	3-4	Soy sauce	2 tbsps
Cornstarch	2 tbsps	Ajinomoto	¼ tsp
Mushrooms	10-12	White pepper powder	½ tsp
Ginger	1 inch piece	Salt	to taste
Garlic	2-3 cloves	Vegetable stock	2 cups

METHOD OF PREPARATION

1 Clean, wash and soak rice in four to five cups of water for an hour. Boil rice in sufficient water with star anise until just cooked. Remove, drain well, transfer rice to clay pot and keep warm.

2 Soak oyster mushrooms in sufficient hot water for fifteen minutes, drain, roughly chop. Blend cornstarch in half a cup of water.

3 Clean, wash, trim and slice mushrooms. Wash, peel and grate ginger. Peel and finely chop garlic. Wash, trim and finely chop spring onions and reserve some chopped spring onion greens for garnish.

4 Heat oil in a wok, add grated ginger, chopped garlic and stir fry briefly. Add chopped spring onions and continue to stir fry for a minute.

5 Add soy sauce, oyster mushrooms, ajinomoto, white pepper powder, salt to taste and stir in vegetable stock. Bring to a boil, add sliced mushrooms and stir in blended cornstarch.

6 Cook for a minute or until the sauce thickens, stirring continuously. Pour the sauce on the rice, cover with a lid and keep in a pre-heated oven at 180 degree Celsius for twelve to fifteen minutes.

7 Open the pot at the dining table, stir well, garnish with the reserved spring onion greens and serve hot.

Note : *Refer page no.130 for the recipe of Vegetable Stock.*

SICHUAN VEGETABLE FRIED RICE

INGREDIENTS

Rice .... 1 cup	Oil .... 6 tbsps
Spring onions 2	Red chilli paste .... 1 tbsp
Ginger .... 1 inch piece	Ajinomoto .... ¼ tsp
Garlic .... 4-6 cloves	White pepper powder .... ¼ tsp
Carrot .... 1 medium sized	Salt .... to taste
French beans 4-6	Vinegar .... 1 tbsp
Red chillies whole 3-4	

METHOD OF PREPARATION

1 Clean, wash and soak rice in four to five cups of water for an hour. Cook in sufficient boiling water until just cooked. Remove, drain well and cool.

2 Wash, trim, finely chop spring onions and reserve some chopped greens for garnish. Wash, peel and finely chop ginger. Peel and finely chop garlic.

3 Wash, peel and finely chop carrot. Wash, string and finely chop French beans. Remove stem and break red chillies into two.

4 Heat oil in a wok, add broken red chillies, chopped garlic, ginger, spring onion and stir fry briefly.

5 Add carrot, beans and continue to stir fry for a minute. Add red chilli paste, ajinomoto, white pepper powder, salt to taste and mix well.

6 Add rice and cook on high heat for a minute or until the rice is heated through, tossing continuously. Mix in vinegar and serve hot, garnished with chopped spring onion greens.

Burnt Ginger Rice (Page 115), Pot Mushroom Rice (Page 111) & Sichuan Vegetable Fried Rice (Page 112) ▶

BURNT GINGER RICE

INGREDIENTS

Rice	1 cup	Tomato sauce	½ tbsp
Onion	1 small sized	Red chilli paste	½ tbsp
Ginger	four 1 inch pieces	Ajinomoto	¼ tsp
Coriander leaves	2-3 sprigs	Salt	to taste
Oil	6 tbsps	Vinegar	1 tbsp
Light soy sauce	1 tbsp		

METHOD OF PREPARATION

1. Clean, wash and soak rice in four to five cups of water for an hour. Cook in sufficient boiling water until just cooked. Remove, drain well and cool.

2. Peel, wash and finely chop onion. Wash, peel and thinly slice ginger. Wash, trim and chop coriander leaves.

3. Heat oil in a wok, add sliced ginger and stir fry for two to three minutes or until the ginger turns brown in colour. Remove with a slotted spoon and drain onto an absorbent kitchen towel. Reserve some ginger pieces for garnish and finely chop the remaining ginger.

4. Reheat oil, add chopped fried ginger, onion and stir fry briefly. Immediately add cooked rice, light soy sauce, tomato sauce, red chilli paste, ajinomoto and salt to taste.

5. Cook on high heat for a minute, stirring and tossing continuously. Add chopped coriander leaves, vinegar and serve hot, garnished with reserved fried ginger slices.

Chef's Tip : *Left over steamed rice can be used for preparing fried rice.*

BEST OF CHINESE COOKING

◀ *Vegetable Hakka Noodles (Page 116)*

VEGETABLE HAKKA NOODLES

INGREDIENTS

Noodles .... 400 gms	Oil.. 6 tbsps
Onion .... 1 medium sized	Soy sauce .... 1 tbsp
Spring onions greens 1	Ajinomoto.......................... ¼ tsp
Capsicum .... 1 medium sized	Salt................................to taste
Carrot.................... 1 medium sized	White pepper powder .... ¼ tsp
Cabbage.................... ¼ small sized	Bean sprouts.....................1 cup

METHOD OF PREPARATION

1 Boil noodles in sufficient water. Drain, remove and cool. Peel, wash and slice onion. Wash, trim and finely shred spring onions greens.

2 Wash, halve, deseed and cut capsicum into julienne. Wash, peel and cut carrot into julienne. Wash, trim, remove core and finely shred cabbage.

3 Heat oil in a wok, add sliced onion and stir fry briefly. Add carrot, capsicum, cabbage and stir fry for two minutes, stirring and tossing continuously.

4 Add noodles, soy sauce, ajinomoto, salt to taste, white pepper powder and cook on high heat for a couple of minutes or until the noodles are heated through, tossing continuously.

5 Add bean sprouts, mix well and serve hot garnished with chopped spring onion greens.

Chef's Tip : *It is a practice to add French beans in Vegetable Hakka Noodles, however I have omitted them because my younger daughter does not like it!*

CHICKEN FRIED RICE

INGREDIENTS

Rice	1 cup	Salt	to taste
Chicken (boneless)	100 gms	Soy sauce	1 tbsp
Spring onions	2	Ajinomoto	¼ tsp
Garlic	3-4 cloves	White pepper powder	½ tsp
Eggs	2	Vinegar	½ tbsp
Oil	4 tbsps		

METHOD OF PREPARATION

1   Clean, wash and soak rice in four to five cups of water for an hour. Cook in sufficient boiling water until just cooked. Remove, drain well and cool.

2   Clean and cut chicken into thin strips. Wash, trim and finely chop spring onions. Peel and finely chop garlic. Break eggs in a bowl and whisk lightly.

3   Heat oil in a wok, add chopped spring onions, garlic and stir fry briefly. Add chicken pieces and stir fry for two minutes. Add lightly beaten eggs and cook for half a minute, stirring continuously.

4   Add cooked rice and salt, cook for a minute, stirring and tossing continuously. Add soy sauce, ajinomoto, white pepper powder and mix thoroughly.

5   Add vinegar, mix well and serve hot.

SESAME HOT NOODLES

INGREDIENTS

Noodles	400 gms	Chilli sauce	4 tbsps
Sesame oil	2 tbsps	Ajinomoto	¼ tsp
Spring onions	2	White pepper powder	½ tsp
Green chillies	2	Salt	to taste
Garlic	3-4 cloves	Sesame seeds (toasted)	2 tbsps
Peanuts (roasted)	½ cup	Bean sprouts	1 cup
Oil	4 tbsps	Vinegar	1 tbsp
Light soy sauce	3 tbsps		

METHOD OF PREPARATION

1   Boil noodles in sufficient water. Remove, drain well and mix in sesame oil.

2   Wash, trim and slice spring onions. Wash, remove stem and finely chop green chillies. Peel and finely chop garlic. Lightly crush roasted peanuts.

3   Heat oil in a wok, add chopped garlic, green chillies, sliced spring onions and stir fry briefly. Add boiled noodles, light soy sauce, chilli sauce, ajinomoto, white pepper powder, salt to taste and continue to stir fry for a couple of minutes.

4   Add crushed peanuts, toasted sesame seeds, bean sprouts, vinegar and cook on a high heat for a minute, stirring and tossing continuously. Serve hot.

Chef's Tip : *Add a tablespoon of oil while boiling the noodles to prevent them from sticking together.*

SHANGHAI STEWED NOODLES

INGREDIENTS

Noodles .... 200 gms	Cornstarch .... 1½ tbsps
Onion .... 1 medium sized	Oil .... 1 tbsp
Spring onions greens 1	Vegetable stock .... 5 cups
Garlic .... 6-8 cloves	Ajinomoto .... ¼ tsp
Capsicum .... ½ medium sized	White pepper powder ...... ½ tsp
Carrot .... ½ medium sized	Salt .... to taste
Mushrooms 4	Chilli oil .... 2 tbsps
Cabbage .... ¼ small sized	

METHOD OF PREPARATION

1   Peel, wash and slice onion. Wash, trim and slice spring onion greens. Peel and crush garlic. Wash, deseed and cut capsicum into bite sized pieces.

2   Wash, peel, halve and cut carrot into slices. Clean, wash and slice mushrooms. Wash, trim, remove core and cut cabbage into bite sized pieces. Blend cornstarch in half a cup of water.

3   Heat oil in a wok, add the crushed garlic, sliced onion and stir fry briefly. Add carrot, mushroom, cabbage, capsicum and continue to stir fry for a minute.

4   Add vegetable stock, bring to a boil and add noodles. Cook on high heat for two minutes, reduce heat and simmer for four to five minutes or until noodles are almost cooked.

5   Stir in ajinomoto, white pepper powder, salt to taste and blended cornstarch. Cook on medium heat for a couple of minutes or until the sauce thickens, stirring frequently.

6   Add spring onion greens, drizzle chilli oil and serve hot.

Note : *Refer page no.130 for the recipe of Vegetable Stock.*

SINGAPORE NOODLE RICE

INGREDIENTS

Rice .... ¾ cup	Chilli oil .... 4 tbsps
Noodles .... 100 gms	Soy sauce .... ½ tbsp
Chicken (boneless) ...... 200 gms	Tomato sauce .... 3 tbsps
Prawns (shelled) ... 12 small sized	Ajinomoto .... ¼ tsp
Spring onions 2	White pepper powder ...... ½ tsp
Ginger .... 1 inch piece	Salt .... to taste
Garlic .... 3-4 cloves	Vinegar .... 1 tbsp
Eggs 2	

METHOD OF PREPARATION

1   Clean, wash and soak rice in four to five cups of water for an hour. Cook in sufficient boiling water until just cooked. Remove, drain well and cool.

2   Wash, trim, finely chop spring onions and reserve some chopped greens for garnish. Wash, peel and finely chop ginger. Peel and finely chop garlic. Break eggs into a bowl and whisk lightly.

3   Boil noodles in sufficient water. Drain, remove and cool. Wash and cut chicken into thin strips. Devein, wash thoroughly and pat dry prawns with an absorbent kitchen towel.

4   Heat chilli oil in a wok, add chopped garlic, ginger and stir fry briefly. Add chicken pieces, prawns and continue to stir fry for half a minute. Add chopped spring onions and cook on high heat for a minute more.

5   Stir in whisked egg and continue to cook on high heat for half a minute or until the egg is scrambled.

6   Add noodles, rice, soy sauce, tomato sauce, ajinomoto, white pepper powder and salt to taste. Mix well and cook for a couple of minutes until noodles and rice are heated through, tossing continuously.

7   Mix in vinegar and serve hot, garnished with chopped spring onion greens.

AMERICAN CHOPSUEY

INGREDIENTS

Noodles	300 gms	Cornstarch	2 tbsps
Chicken (boneless)	100 gms	Eggs	4
Oil	6 tbsps + to deep fry	Tomato sauce	½ cup
Onion	1 medium sized	Soy sauce	½ tbsp
Carrot	½ medium sized	White pepper powder	½ tsp
French beans	3-4	Ajinomoto	¼ tsp
Cabbage	¼ small sized	Salt	to taste
Capsicum	½ medium sized	Chicken stock	2 cups
Ginger	1 inch piece	Vinegar	1 tbsp
Garlic	3-4 cloves	Bean sprouts	½ cup

METHOD OF PREPARATION

1 Boil noodles until almost cooked, drain, remove and cool. Heat sufficient oil in a wok and deep fry noodles till crisp and golden brown in colour. Remove and drain onto an absorbent kitchen towel. Divide the fried noodles into four equal portions and keep warm in separate shallow plates or serving platter.

2 Clean and cut chicken into thin strips. Peel, wash and finely slice onion. Wash, peel and cut carrot into julienne. Wash, string and cut French beans diagonally into julienne.

3 Wash, remove core and finely shred cabbage. Wash, deseed and cut capsicum into julienne. Wash, peel and grate ginger. Peel and finely chop garlic. Blend cornstarch in half a cup of water.

4 Heat a non stick pan with half a tablespoon of oil, break an egg, cook for half a minute on both sides. Repeat this to make four such double fried eggs.

5 Heat four tablespoons of oil in a wok or a pan, add chopped garlic, grated ginger and stir fry briefly. Add chicken and cook for half a minute. Add sliced onion, carrot, French beans, cabbage and continue to stir fry for a minute.

6 Add tomato sauce, soy sauce, white pepper powder, ajinomoto, salt to taste, capsicum and stir in the chicken stock. Cook for two minutes and stir in the blended cornstarch. Continue to cook for a minute or until the sauce thickens.

7 Add vinegar, bean sprouts, stir well and pour over the fried noodles.

8 Serve hot with each portion of American Chopsuey topped with double fried egg.

Note : *Refer page no.129 for the recipe of Chicken Stock.*

DAARSAAN

INGREDIENTS

Wonton skins 16-20	Honey .... 1/4 cup
Oil .... to deep fry	Sesame seeds (toasted) ...... 2 tbsps
Butter................................... 1 tbsp	Icing sugar .... 2 tbsps
Sugar .... 1/4 cup	

METHOD OF PREPARATION

1 Make eight to ten long cuts on the wonton skins leaving the edges intact. Moisten top and bottom edges, roll loosely as you would roll a toffee wrapper. Pinch the ends to secure.

2 Heat sufficient oil in a wok and deep fry prepared wontons skins for a minute or until crisp and golden brown in colour. Remove, drain onto an absorbent kitchen towel and transfer to a shallow serving dish. Keep warm.

3 Heat butter in a pan with one tablespoon of water and sugar. Continue cooking until sugar melts and turns light golden brown.

4 Reduce heat and stir in the honey and pour the sauce on crisp fried wonton skins.

5 Sprinkle toasted sesame seeds, icing sugar and serve warm.

Chef's Tip : *You can make Daarsaan using flat noodles as well. Serve Daarsaan with ice cream of your choice.*

122

DATE AND WALNUT WONTONS

INGREDIENTS

Seedless dates .... 100 gms	Cinnamon powder............ ¼ tsp
Walnuts kernels .... ½ cup	Wonton skins.........................16
Brown sugar .... 2 tbsps	Oil .... to deep fry

METHOD OF PREPARATION

1 Clean and finely chop seedless dates. Boil walnut kernels in two cups of water for a minute. Drain and remove. Pat dry walnuts with an absorbent kitchen towel and roughly chop.

2 Mix chopped dates, walnuts, brown sugar and cinnamon powder. Divide the date mixture into sixteen equal portions.

3 Place a portion of date and walnut mixture in the center of each wonton wrapper, wet the edges with a little water, fold into half and twist the ends and stick.

4 Heat sufficient oil in a wok, add stuffed wontons and deep fry for a couple of minutes or until golden brown and crisp.

5 Remove and drain onto an absorbent kitchen towel. Serve hot with ice cream of your choice.

TOFFEE APPLE

INGREDIENTS

Apples .... 4 medium sized	Oil................................. to deep fry
Cornstarch .... 4 tbsps	Butter .... 1 tbsp
Refined flour .... 1 cup	Sugar... ½ cup
Baking powder...................... ½ tsp	Sesame seeds (toasted)........ 1 tbsp

METHOD OF PREPARATION

1 Peel, core, cut apples into quarters and cut each quarter lengthwise in half. Coat apple segments thoroughly in two tablespoons of cornstarch, shaking off excess.

2 Sieve refined flour, remaining cornstarch and baking powder. Gradually stir in the one and quarter cup of water to make a smooth batter.

3 Heat sufficient oil in a wok, dip cornstarch coated apple segments into batter and deep fry in hot oil for about a minute or until golden brown, turning them occasionally. Remove and drain onto an absorbent kitchen towel, keep warm.

4 Heat butter in a pan with two tablespoons of water and sugar. Continue cooking until sugar melts and turns light golden brown.

5 Remove from heat and dip fried apple pieces into prepared hot caramel. Sprinkle toasted sesame seeds and dip in iced water to harden the crust. Immediately remove and serve.

Chef's Tip : *You can also make toffees with banana, lychee or any other fruit of your choice.*

CARAMEL BANANA

INGREDIENTS

Bananas (ripe)	8	Sugar	½ cup
Cornstarch	4 tbsps	Honey	4 tbsps
Butter	3 tbsps	Sesame seeds (toasted)	2 tbsps

METHOD OF PREPARATION

1 Peel and slice banana into two horizontally. Cut each half into two and roll in cornstarch.

2 Heat two tablespoons of butter in a pan, add cornstarch coated bananas and pan fry for a minute or until light brown in colour. Turn over the banana pieces and continue to fry for a minute more. Remove and transfer to a shallow serving dish. Keep warm.

3 Heat a pan, add sugar and remaining butter and cook on medium heat without stirring till it is melted and starts to change colour.

4 Stir with a wooden spoon till the sugar has caramelized to a light golden colour. Reduce heat and stir in the honey.

5 Mix well and pour hot sauce over the pan fried bananas. Sprinkle toasted sesame seeds and serve immediately.

Chef's Tip : *Select sweet and firm bananas for best results. You can replace banana with other fruits like apple, pineapple, pear, peach and mango.*

STEAMED DATE BUNS

INGREDIENTS

Dough
Refined flour .... 450 gms
Sugar .... 3 tsps
Dry yeast .... 1½ tbsps
Milk .... ½ cup
Salt .... ¼ tsp

Sesame oil .... 1 tbsp
Filling
Seedless dates .... 125 gms
Walnut kernels .... ½ cup
Butter .... 1 tbsp
Sweet bean paste .... 2 tbsps

METHOD OF PREPARATION

1. Dissolve the sugar and dry yeast in lukewarm milk and leave aside for fifteen minutes or until frothy.

2. Sieve the refined flour and salt together, make a well in the center, add the yeast mixture and make a soft dough adding enough water.

3. Add sesame oil and knead the dough with your palm and leave aside in a warm place for fifteen minutes or until it doubles in size. Knock out the air bubbles by kneading once again and divide into sixteen equal portions.

4. Meanwhile clean and finely chop the dates. Wipe and roughly chop the walnuts.

5. Heat the butter in a pan and stir in the bean paste diluted in two tablespoons of water.

6. Add the dates and walnuts and cook for two minutes till it starts leaving the sides of the pan. Remove from heat and cool.

7. Roll each portion of the dough into two inch round discs, place a portion of the filling and gather the sides to form into a ball.

8. Rest the prepared buns covered with a moist cloth for five minutes. Place in bamboo steamers and steam on high heat for fifteen minutes or until completely cooked.

9. Serve hot straight from the steamer.

CHICKEN STOCK

INGREDIENTS

Chicken bones .... 200 gms	Parsley .... 2-3 stalks
Onion .... 1 medium sized	Peppercorns 6-7
Carrot .... 1 medium sized	Cloves 5-6
Celery .... 1 stalk	Bayleaf 1
Leek 1	

METHOD OF PREPARATION

1 Wash and clean bones, remove any excess fat. Heat sufficient water in a pan and put the bones in it and boil for five minutes. Drain and remove the bones.

2 Peel, wash and cut onion into quarters. Wash and cut carrot into two-three large pieces. Wash and cut celery, leek and parsley stalks into one-two inch pieces. Wash leek leaves.

3 Put blanched bones, onion, carrot, celery, parsley, leek, leek leaves, peppercorns, cloves and bayleaf in a stockpot (deep pan) with ten cups of water and heat. Bring the stock to boil. Remove any scum which comes on the top and replace it with more cold water. Simmer the stock for a minimum period of one hour.

4 Remove from heat, strain, cool and store in a refrigerator till further use.

Chef's Tip : *Unutilised chicken carcass (neck, winglets, bones, etc.) can be used to make this stock.*

VEGETABLE STOCK

INGREDIENTS

Onion .... 1 medium sized
Carrot .... ½ medium sized
Celery.................... 2-3 inch stalk
Garlic..................................2 cloves

Bayleaf 1
Peppercorns 5-6
Cloves 2-3

METHOD OF PREPARATION

1 Peel, wash and slice onion and carrot. Wash and cut celery into small pieces. Peel and crush garlic.

2 Take all the ingredients in a pan with five cups of water and bring it to a boil.

3 Simmer for fifteen minutes and strain. Cool and store in a refrigerator till further use.

FISH STOCK

INGREDIENTS

Fish bones, head, skin ..... 200 gms	Mushroom .... 1 large
Onion .... 1 medium sized	Bay leaf 1
Celery .... 2-3 inch stalk	Peppercorns 4-6

METHOD OF PREPARATION

1. Peel, wash and slice onion, wash and cut celery into one centimeter pieces, wash and slice mushroom.

2. In a pan put fish bones, head, skin (any unutilised portion of fish), five cups of water, onion slices, mushroom slices, celery pieces, bayleaf and peppercorns and put it on heat.

3. Bring it to boil, remove any scum, which comes on top and then simmer for fifteen minutes. Remove from heat, strain and use the liquid as stock.

Chef's Tip : *Fish stock should not be stored in the refrigerator as it smells and affects other food.*

CHILLI GARLIC SAUCE

INGREDIENTS

Red chillies whole	20	Sugar	1 tbsp
Garlic	8 cloves	Salt	to taste
Vinegar	8 tbsps	Sesame oil	1 ½ tbsps

METHOD OF PREPARATION

1. Mix all the ingredients except oil and blend to a fine paste in a mixer.
2. Add oil and blend well.
3. Keep refrigerated.

BLACK BEAN SAUCE

INGREDIENTS

Black beans	3 tbsps	Vinegar	2 tbsps
Vegetable stock	¾ cup	Soy sauce	1 tbsp
Cornstarch	2 tsps	Salt	to taste
Ginger	½ inch piece	Pepper powder	to taste
Garlic	1 clove	Sugar	1 tsp

METHOD OF PREPARATION

1   Soak the black beans overnight. Boil till soft.
2   Peel, wash and roughly chop ginger and garlic. Mix the cornstarch in a little vegetable stock and keep aside.
3   Mix black beans, ginger, garlic, vinegar, soy sauce, salt, pepper powder, sugar and remaining vegetable stock and blend in a mixer.
4   Transfer to a pan, add the cornstarch mixture and mix well. Simmer until thick.

SICHUAN SAUCE

INGREDIENTS

Red chillies whole	10-12	Oil	½ cup
Green chillies	2	Vegetable stock or water	½ cup
Spring onions	2	Tomato ketchup	3 tbsps
Ginger	1 inch piece	Salt	to taste
Garlic	10 cloves	Vinegar	2 tsps
Celery	2-3 inch stalk		

METHOD OF PREPARATION

1 Remove the stems, wash and finely chop the green chillies. Peel, wash and finely chop the spring onions. Wash and finely chop some of the spring onion greens. Peel, wash and grate the ginger. Peel, wash and finely chop two cloves of garlic. Wash and cut celery stalk into small pieces. Remove stems and boil whole red chillies in one cup of water for five to seven minutes.

2 Grind the whole red chillies and the remaining cloves of garlic to a fine paste.

3 Heat oil, add chopped garlic, green chillies, spring onions and grated ginger and sauté for a minute.

4 Add the red chillies and garlic paste and continue to sauté.

5 Add vegetable stock or water, celery, tomato ketchup, salt and stir to blend well. Add vinegar and chopped spring onion greens.

6 Simmer for a minute and take off the heat. Cool and store.

Note : *Refer page no.130 for the recipe of Vegetable Stock.*

SWEET CORIANDER SAUCE

INGREDIENTS

Coriander leaves	3½ tbsps	Salt	to taste
Garlic	3 cloves	Pepper powder	½ tsp
Cornstarch	1 tbsp	Sugar	⅓ cup
Oil	1 tsp	Lemon juice	2 tsps

METHOD OF PREPARATION

1 Clean, wash and finely chop the coriander leaves. Peel and finely chop the garlic. Mix the cornstarch in half a cup of water and keep aside.

2 Heat oil, add the chopped garlic and sauté for a minute.

3 Add one cup of water, chopped coriander leaves, salt, pepper powder, sugar and lemon juice and stir to mix well.

4 When the mixture begins to boil, reduce heat and add the cornstarch mixed in water.

5 Stir and simmer till sauce thickens. Cool and store.

SWEET AND SOUR SAUCE

INGREDIENTS

Tomato ketchup .... 1 cup

Malt vinegar .... $^1/_3$ cup

Soy sauce .... 2 tsps

Sugar .... $^1/_4$ cup

Pepper powder .... to taste

Salt .... to taste

Cornstarch .... 2 tbsps

METHOD OF PREPARATION

1 Mix all the ingredients in a pan with two cups of water and stir to blend well.

2 Slowly heat the mixture, stirring continuously till it comes to a boil.

3 Reduce heat and simmer for two to three minutes.

4 Cool and store.

Note : *Plain vinegar can be used.*

AJINOMOTO/MONOSODIUM GLUTAMATE OR MSG : Flavour enhancer widely used in Chinese and Japanese cooking along with other seasonings. It is extracted from seaweed and other vegetable matter. Flavour enhancing secret of this seaweed is an amino acid called glutamate. Its use is optional and it is best used sparingly.

BAMBOO SHOOTS : These are the tender spear shaped shoots from the base of bamboo plants. When using the canned ones, rinse in hot water before use. Unused portions should be kept in water in the refrigerator and water should be changed regularly.

BAMBOO STEAMER : A special kind of steamer made from bamboo strips used in Chinese cooking specially for steaming dimsums. These are round and lidded containers, which can be stacked one on top of the other. They are placed over boiling water so that steam filters through the holes in the bamboo and gently cooks the food.

BEAN CURD : Also known as Dou Fu in Chinese and Tofu in Japanese, it is made with boiled soya bean liquid. It is soft and white, cheese-like in texture, ranges from firm to silken. It is high in protein and low in fat. Highly nutritious and bland in flavour, it mixes well with other ingredients. Can be stored upto three weeks in the refrigerator.

BEAN SPROUTS : Bean sprouts are sprouted green gram (*moong*) and are highly nutritious. Crunchy in texture and nutty in flavour they can be eaten raw but they can also be lightly cooked.

BLACK BEAN FERMENTED : These beans are aromatic and are cooked either only with salt or with salt, ginger and orange peel. Before using them, salt should be rinsed off. However they are not easily available in India.

BLACK BEAN SAUCE : Used in place of soy sauce when a thicker sauce is required. Made from salted soya beans, ground and mixed with flour and spices.

BROCCOLI : Similar to cauliflower, dark green in colour. The word brocco means sprout. In Europe in the early sixties it was referred to as Poor Man's Cauliflower!

BROWN SUGAR : Small crystals of refined white sugar treated with dark grade molasses. Soft light brown sugar is treated with light coloured molasses.

CELERY : A shoot vegetable with a distinct sharp and savoury flavour. The stalk is used to flavour soups and salads. Mildly pungent leaves can also be used as herb.

CELLOPHANE NOODLES : Cellophane noodles are made from green gram flour. They are very hard and fine. Also known as transparent noodles or bean threads. They are sold in bundles. They should be soaked in hot water for five minutes before using, when they become translucent. They are never eaten on their own but combined with soups.

CHILLI OIL : It is a very spicy bright red oil made of chillies with oil. It is also known as chilli pepper oil or hot chilli oil and is used to season dipping sauces and also in cooking.

CHILLI SAUCE : Red or green chilli sauce is available in the market. It is made from chillies ground with vinegar, starch and salt. Occasionally flavoured with garlic, it has thick consistency like tomato sauce and is very hot.

CHINESE BAR-BE-CUE SAUCE : A combination of hoisin sauce, vinegar, sesame oil or paste and bean sauce. Used in marination.

CHINESE CABBAGE : Large headed cabbage with firmly packed pale green leaves. Rich in Vitamin C and other nutrients. Eaten raw in salad, used in stir-fries and soups and for lining bamboo steamers. Chinese cabbage is also wrongly referred to as Bok Choy.

CILANTRO : Leaves of coriander plant, also referred to as Chinese parsley. Used as a garnish. Although it resembles flat leaf parsley in appearance, coriander (cilantro) tastes quite different. While purchasing make sure that it is bright green in colour, has no yellow spots and is not wilting.

CORNSTARCH : Commonly referred to as cornflour. Corn (maize) is processed to eliminate all but the pure starch content. Blended with water to form paste, it is used as a thickening agent.

DRY SHERRY :

Traditional fortified wine. Largely used in cooking, marinating and its sweet version is used in making desserts.

EGG NOODLES, FRESH :

These yellow noodles range in size and shape from long spaghetti like, to thin vermicelli like strands. They can be frozen upto three months or else should be used up within three days of making them.

FERMENTED BEAN CURD :

Also called bean curd cheese, it is made by fermenting small cubes of bean curd in wine and salt. Available in two forms – red and white. Both are salty, with a strong flavour and are used for seasoning meat and vegetables in Chinese cuisine or as a condiment.

FISH SAUCE :

It is a salty, thin, brown liquid made by fermenting fish/shrimps with salt and soy sauce. It is used in place of salt as a seasoning. Made from salted fish, it is rich in Vitamin B and protein. Used in cooking and dipping. Can be stored indefinitely without refrigeration.

FIVE SPICE POWDER :

Aromatic seasoning, which despite its name, can be made from varying combinations of star anise, fennel, cloves, cinnamon, ginger, nutmeg and Sichuan peppercorns ground together. Use sparingly. Store in airtight containers.

GINGER :

This potato coloured root is indispensable to Chinese cooking. Ideally it should have smooth outer skins and since it roughens and wrinkles if kept outside it should be stored in the refrigerator.

HOISIN SAUCE : It is a thick and brownish red sauce. It is made from soya beans, sugar, salt, garlic and chillies with sesame oil. Sometimes vinegar and flour are also used. It is used as a condiment. Another variety is sweet and spicy made from soya bean paste flavoured with garlic, sugar, chillies and other spices. Used in cooking or as a dipping sauce. It is also used to glaze roasted meat. It needs refrigeration.

HOT MUSTARD : Condiment served with Chinese appetizers. Made by mixing dry mustard powder with water, causing a chemical reaction that produces a sharp hot taste. Sesame oil and rice vinegar may also be added.

JULIENNE : Vegetables, like carrots, capsicums or even ginger cut into long thin strips.

LEMON GRASS : A sub tropical plant resembling spring onion which gives a delicious lemony flavour to South East Asian dishes. Bulb may be ground in spice mixtures, the leaves are bruised or sliced and cooked in sauces or used as an aromatic garnish.

LEMON RIND : Lemon peels with the inner white membrane removed can be used, grated or julienned, to garnish dishes both sweet and savoury.

LETTUCE : There are three varieties of lettuce – crisp-head, romaine butter-head or cabbage. All are mainly used raw and in salads, though they can also be cooked. They are available all year round.

LOTUS ROOT : Crunchy and gourd shaped, lotus roots grow underwater, four to five together strung like sausages and often four to five inches long.

MOREL MUSHROOMS : These are the most expensive of the dried mushrooms. But only a few should be used as they add quite a lot of flavour. Dried morels can be added to sauces or rice dishes.

MUSHROOMS : Chinese mushrooms called Shitake are a beautiful pale gold colour when fresh and have a pleasantly firm texture and a haunting flavour. Available dry and should be soaked before cooking. They have a stronger flavour than the fresh ones. Remove stems and store at room temperature. They last indefinitely. Good for people suffering from high blood pressure.

MUSHROOMS, BLACK : Usually available dried, the caps are thick with a nice curl and range in colour from black to speckled brown black. Their sizes range from one-fourth inch to three inches in diameter and are quite expensive.

MUSSELS : A seafood, closely related to the clam, mussels are found the world over on sea shores and are also commercially bred. Mussels are generally sold fresh in their shells and eaten raw or steamed or used in salads or soups.

NOODLES : Noodles is a Chinese staple food. Mein is the generic term after which the popular dish Chow Mein is named. Some are made from hard (durum) wheat (like the Italian pasta) with water or also with eggs and are usually sold in dried form. Some are made from rice while some others from green gram (*moong*).

ORANGE RIND : Dry peels of oranges, julienned, used for garnishing in various sweet and savoury dishes.

OYSTER SAUCE : A dark brown sauce with a rich flavour made from the extract of oysters, salt and starch, used mainly in south of China. Store refrigerated.

PEANUT BUTTER : A paste made from crushed peanuts, used mainly as a spread. Sometimes it is also used to thicken sauces.

PLUM SAUCE : A thick, rich, spicy fruit sauce it is used in savoury braised dishes or in dips. It is available bottled.

RICE NOODLES : Rice noodles are made in southern China from rice flour. They are flat, ribbon like strands that do not require soaking before use. They may be sold in bundles or curled up in a pad.

RICE VINEGAR : Light and delicately flavoured vinegar. Rice vinegar is distilled from white rice and is very aromatic. It is milder than wine or cider vinegar. A good substitute is distilled white vinegar diluted with water. Seasoned rice vinegar with sugar and ajinomoto is also available.

RICE WINE : Wine from fermented rice, it is golden yellow in colour and also known as yellow wine. It has a dry sherry like flavour and is used to flavour many Chinese dishes. It is consistently high in alcoholic content.

SHALLOTS :

Unknown in ancient times and of uncertain origin, it is less pungent than onion. Mainly used in sauces, the elongated variety tends to be stronger in flavour.

SHRIMPS :

Another type of seafood. There are several varieties of shrimps, which reach a maximum of four inches in length. Pale pink when raw, shrimps are available fresh, frozen or canned.

SHRIMP PASTE :

Often used in dishes of vegetables and soups, it is salty in taste and should be used sparingly. Sold in jars and cans, should be refrigerated once opened.

SICHUAN PEPPER :

This spice is not a species of pepper, though it does have a peppery taste. It is added to cooked dishes, and also served mixed with salt as a table condiment.

SNOW PEAS :

Also known as Mangetout. Early varieties of peas, which have very tender pods. They have to be only topped and tailed before cooking and are eaten pod and all. Always look for crisp pods with small peas.

SOY SAUCE :

It is made from fermented soy beans, salt, yeast and sugar. Available in two versions – Dark and Light. Dark soy sauce, thicker and more full bodied, is dark brown and its taste is sweeter. Light soy sauce is thinner and of much paler brownish amber colour. It has a pronounced flavour and is more salty than the darker version.

SOYA BEAN PASTE : Ground soya beans are seasoned and flavoured with chillies, peppers, sugar and salt. A popular addition to highly spiced dishes, especially in western China, it is very hot and aromatic. Called Dou ban jiang in China, it is sold in jars or cans and stays for a long time, especially if refrigerated.

SQUIDS : This seafood is found world wide in temperate waters. They are available fresh or frozen. Smaller squids can be sautéed, poached, broiled or grilled whereas the larger ones are often stewed.

STICKY RICE : Despite its name this rice, widely used in Chinese cooking, is completely gluten free. When boiled it becomes sweet and sticky.

STIR-FRY : To cook small pieces of food in very little fat, tossing constantly over high heat, usually in a wok.

STOCK : It is an aromatic and nutritive liquid extracted by boiling bones, spices and/or vegetables with water. It can be stored in the refrigerator in large quantities and frozen.

SWEET SOYA BEAN PASTE : One of the most popular sweet mixtures with Chinese cooks, it is used in various ways. Sweet soya

WATER CHESTNUT : bean paste is sold in jars or cans and should be refrigerated once opened.

WATER CHESTNUT : It's a walnut sized bulb with brown or green skin. Inside the flesh is white and crisp. Water chestnut flour too is used.

WHITE WINE VINEGAR : Wine vinegars are ideal for mayonnaise and all kinds of salad dressings. They are also used in many sauces that can be served with fish.

WOK : Cone shaped utensil which is normally used to cook Chinese food. It has a rounded bottom, which encourages ingredients to return to the centre.

WONTON WRAPPERS : Wafer thin wrappers eight centimeter (three inches) square made from wheat flour, egg and water. They are usually filled with a savoury mixture and then steamed, deep-fried or boiled. Served with piquant dip sauce. Can be stored in freezer for upto six months. Can be thawed easily and fast.

Subscribe to the most acclaimed food site
www.sanjeevkapoor.com **and avail of unbelievable offers!!!**

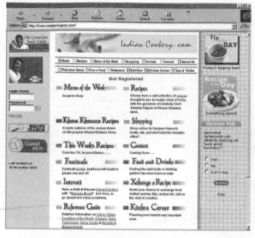

Pay **Rs.600*** only for one year subscription instead of normal subscription charges of **Rs. 1000/-** and get Sanjeev Kapoor Books worth **Rs. 750/- FREE**
(only upto 30th September, 2003).

You will also have access to more than 1000 recipes other than those published in his books besides many other sections, which will be a rare culinary treat to any food lover. In addition to online contests, etc. you will also have opportunities to win fabulous prizes.

Sanjeev Kapoor also invites all food lovers to participate in the Khana Khazana Quiz and win BIG prizes every week. Watch *Khana Khazana* on Zee TV, answer one simple question based on that day's episode correctly, combine it with a favourite recipe of yours and you can be the lucky winner going places.

*Add Service tax Rs. 48.00

Normal Subscription	You Pay	Plus You Get	You Save
Rs 1,000.	Rs 600 (add service tax Rs. 48/-)	Sanjeev Kapoor's books worth **Rs 750 free.**	Rs 1,150.

*Offer open only up to 30th September, 2003

**Delivery address for free books must be in India.

The three books free with each subscription are

☐ Yes, I would like to subscribe to **www.sanjeevkapoor.com** for one year.

Great Offer from the Khazana of Master Chef Sanjeev Kapoor.

Take your pick of book/books and avail of fantastic discounts.

Number of books	You save
1	Rs.25
2	Rs.100
More than two	Rs.200

Please tick the boxes below to indicate the books you wish to purchase.

Khazana of Indian Recipes	Khazana of Healthy Tasty Recipes	Khana Khazana — Celebration of Indian Cooking	Low Calorie Vegetarian Cookbook	Any Time Temptations	Best of Chinese Cooking	Microwave Cooking Made Easy
MRP: **Rs 250**	MRP: **Rs 250**	MRP: **Rs 250**	MRP: **Rs 250**	MRP: **Rs 225**	MRP: **Rs 250**	MRP: **Rs 250**
☐	☐	☐	☐	☐	☐	☐

I'm enclosing cheque/DD No. _____ dated: _____ for Rs._____

(Rupees in words): _____ only drawn

on (specify bank and branch) _____

favouring **Popular Prakashan Pvt Ltd, Mumbai**

Name: Mr./Ms _____

Address: _____

_____

City: _____ Pin: _____ State: _____

Phone Res: _____ Off: _____ E-mail: _____

Please fill in the coupon in capital letters and mail it with your cheque/DD to :

Popular Prakashan Pvt Ltd,
35-C, Pt Madan Mohan Malaviya Marg, Tardeo, Mumbai – 400 034.
Phone: 022-24941656,24944295 Fax: 022-24945294,
E-mail: info@popularprakashan.com

Delivery subject to realisation of cheque/DD. Offer valid in India only.
Please allow two weeks for processing your subscription. Please superscribe your name and address on the reverse of the cheque/DD.
All disputes are subject to the exclusive jurisdiction of competent courts and forums in Mumbai only.

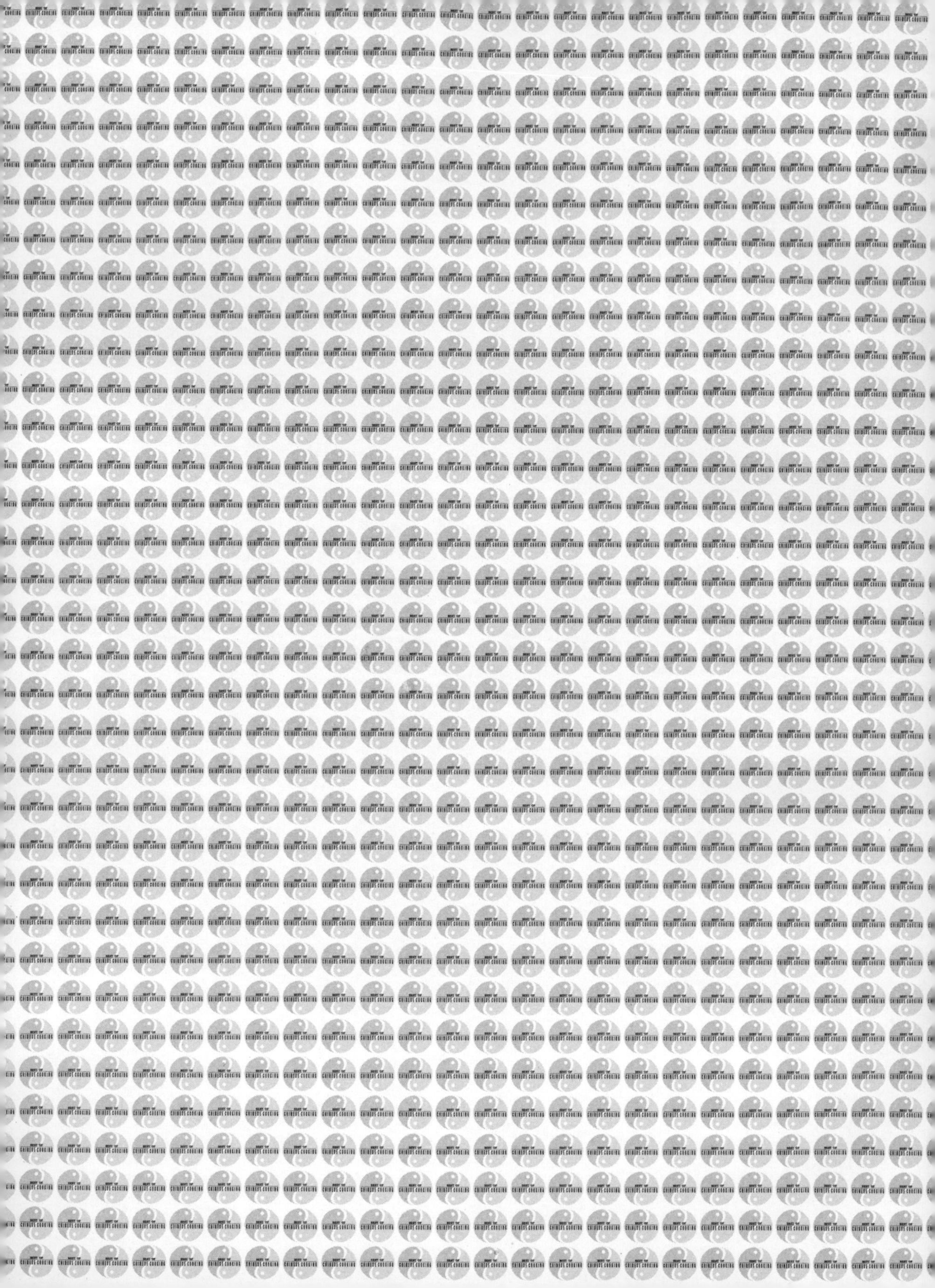
BEST OF
CHINESE COOKING